TEAM HARDEN'S MARRIAGE SURVIVAL Guide

-Lessons We Used To Survive Our Marriage-

Thank you for ordering my book Mrs. Goods. I pray it blesses your life.

By

Clyde E Harden Jr.

Now Available

"The Pastor's Manual, From the Ground Up"

TEAM HARDEN'S MARRIAGE SURVIVAL Guide

-Lessons We Used To Survive Our Marriage-

Copyright

Copyright © 2018 by Clyde E Harden Jr.

All rights reserved. No part of this publication may be reproduced, distributed, or transmitted in any form or by any means, including photocopying, recording, or other electronic or mechanical methods, without the prior written permission of the publisher, except in the case of brief quotations embodied in critical reviews and certain other noncommercial uses permitted by copyright law.

Printed in the United States of America

First Printing, 2018

Dedication

This book is a testament of my marriage. Marriage has been one of the toughest things I have ever done, and I know this is also true for my wife. Then it only became even more challenging after we had our three beautiful daughters. But, they made us who we are today. So, I am dedicating this book to my wife Tonya Harden, and my three daughters Kiaunna, Alana, & Madison.

Tonya, I want you to know how much I love you. I understand that love is more than just words, it is actions. And I pray you understand all of the actions I have done to become a better man for you and our girls is a reflection of how much I appreciate you for being a part of my life. I value you so much, and thank you for having my back over the past 17 years and 9 months at the time this book is being written. You have been a loyal friend, committed wife, dedicated mother, and passionate first lady. I mean it when I say, "God had me in mind when he made you." I want to say thank you for motivating me to be a better me, and inspiring me to become a Man, Husband, Father, Pastor, and now author. I was very hard to live with, I understand that more now than I ever did, but you hung in there. Thank you so much. I only can hope to God that I was half the man to you that you were as a woman to me. You saved my life. Before you I did not know who I was, where I was going, or what my purpose was. You gave me purpose, and direction. Thank you for understanding me.

Kiaunna, my oldest. I love you. You are my first daughter/child. You gave me the push I needed to take my life to another level. When I heard I was going to be a father, I became the happiest man in the world. Once you arrived my happiness doubled. You never cease to amaze me with your tenacity, hard work, and a mind to be the best you can be in all that you do. Thank you for being patient with me as I learned to become a father. You helped me learn what to and not to do. I wasn't a father until I had you, and you helped me become a better one. Thank you for always being willing to step in and help where you can. You are very independent, when I think about you I have no worries or regrets. I know you are going to be ok, you are a survivor. Go, conquer, overcome, and win. That is who you are. I love you.

Alana, my mini me. I love you so much Alana. You remind me so much of myself. From your smart mouth, to your smart mind. We get each other. I want you to know one thing sweet heart, you can have and do whatever you put your mind to. I am proud of who you are, and who you have the potential to become. You came in my life during a time where fight was my middle name. I was fighting to get a better life for my family. You never saw the struggle your sister experienced, but some way you still have a great appreciation for everything. Keep being you, I love you just the way you are.

Last, but not least, my road dog Maddie. Madison Marie Harden, you're like a dream come true. every day I see you, you remind me of genuine love. You genuinely love everyone, especially your mom and me. You make everyone feel special, no matter their age, race, or gender. Your love for me and others has made me a better father. You have shown me the importance of patients. I never knew that until we had you. You slowed me down, and taught me to enjoy life. Your sisters have you to thank when they have me at their games, school programs, and other events. You made me slow down because I wanted to see you grow up. I love you little lady, and thank you for being my Maddie.

I love my entire family, and my New Destiny Family. I thank each you for all that you do for my family. I pray this book helps each of you, and other families around the world.

Table of Contents

INTRODUCTION XI
LESSON 1 *SEPARATE FROM THY MOTHER AND FATHER* 1
LESSON 2 *PUTTING OUR ASSETS TOGETHER* 19
LESSON 3 *CHRIST IS THE ANSWER* 33
LESSON 4 *LET IT ALL HANG OUT* 43
LESSON 5 *SERVING THE RIGHT WAY* 51
LESSON 6 *STAYING TOGETHER* 59
LESSON 7 *IT'S TO LATE, THEY ALREADY FEEL IT* 69
LESSON 8 *TRUTH MOMENT* 79
LESSON 9 *ROMANCE, WITHOUT FINANCE, IS A NUISANCE* 85
LESSON 10 *PARENTING IS A PARTNERSHIP* 97
LESSON 11 *HIS NEEDS HER NEEDS* 107
LESSON 12 *TEAM HARDEN* 115

Introduction

In 1993, I arrived in the small town of Coldspring, Texas, where my father lived. This was the beginning of the rest of my life. Up until this point, I had moved back and forth with my mother and father multiple times, but my mother's recent health issues would cause this to be my last move.

After completing a very successful school year in Cleveland, Texas, my father came to pick me up. On the way home, we stopped by the local grocery store and ran into my cousin. He greeted me with a hug and noticed my bags, then asked if I was moving in with my father. Once I answered him, the next words out of his mouth were, "I have the perfect woman for you." The name that came out of his mouth was Tonya Hines. I did not know, at that time, that this woman would change my life forever.

Only thirteen at the time, I had a lot of life behind me; more than a thirteen-year-old should have ever gone through, but that is another book. Nevertheless, I had my entire life still ahead of me. I never thought this girl my cousin sang praises about would end up being my soulmate, the mother of my kids, the carrier of my dreams, the supporter of my vision, the first lady of my church, and the last lady in my life.

Many late nights, early mornings, and all-day phone conversations later, I finally asked this young lady to be my girlfriend. We dated off and on for the next five years, until finally going our separate ways in 1998, the year she graduated. I must say, this was the best thing that ever happened to our relationship. I like to say that she got a chance to see all the men who weren't for her before she finally realized I was the only man for her. I must admit, though, this was a two-way revelation.

After being separated for more than three years, God touched my heart one day to reach out to her. I was in the military, facing a very low place in life, and it reminded me of the times when my wife and I were broken up in high school, but I still reached out to her for help. That was one thing about our relationship; no matter if we were together or not, she was my best friend; she was always the one I called when I needed help. We just understood one another.

Just a side note: men and women, make sure the one you marry is the one you trust with your life. They need to be your best friend, not just your sex buddy.

Once again, facing a very low place in my life, I did not know who else to call but her. I was unable to contact her immediately, but she eventually got the message that I was looking for her. By God's plan, she reached out to me, once again changing my life forever.

Reigniting our relationship was the help I needed; finally, I had someone who understood me for who I was. Once again, late nights, early mornings, and all-day conversations led me to ask her to marry me. She said yes. SHE SAID YES! I was so excited. I hopped on a plane, flew to Texas in December of 2000, and married her. This was a little wedding with just a few people in attendance, although we planned to have a larger ceremony in May of 2001. We were married, but not living together. I had to return to Virginia without her because I was on active duty in the United States Navy.

I flew back to Texas about five months later to get my wife. After our second ceremony, we were finally able to move together. We were finally about to be able to enjoy our marriage, so we thought. I must say, this was when the fight to survive our marriage began. Almost eighteen years later, at the time of me writing this book, we are still fighting to survive our marriage. Marriage has proven to be one of the hardest things I have ever done in my life. Once you think you have it all figured out, everything changes.

It was only recently that my wife and I decided to write this book. Sitting in a room with our administrators, planning to do what we love to do and help marriages at an upcoming marriage conference, we decided that we wanted to offer a marriage survival guide. A small pamphlet with a few tips we learned over the years in our marriage. After the idea shifted to us brainstorming, we soon understood that all the issues we overcame, all the marriages we helped and lessons we learned could not fit into a small pamphlet. We understood, at that point, the things God allowed our marriage to go through and survive obligated us to write this book.

This book is filled with the greatest survival lessons we learned throughout the years. It has been a bumpy road, to say the least, but we made it up in our mind years ago— not at the altar, but a few years later— that we would not quit. We have had many opportunities, but the lessons and tips we share in this book helped us overcome every obstacle. We know marriage is not something you do and live happily ever after. We have learned that marriage is something you survive. My wife and I like to say, "Marriage is work, but it is worth it."

Even though this book is written by me, a man, and my wife's book is written by her, a woman, we strongly suggest each of you read both books. It will help you understand both perspectives of the marriage. So, sit back, relax, and enjoy the good, bad, and ugly parts of our marriage. We pray our marriage struggles help you succeed at surviving yours.

Lesson 1
Separate from Thy Mother and Father

Over the last three years, I have noticed more and more married couples are living together with one of their parents. Not clearly understanding why, I assumed that this came to be for one of two reasons. One assumption was they must have gotten married with the intention of moving out but were unable to due to unforeseen circumstances. Another assumption was the couple fell on tough times, and the most convenient solution was to move back home for a little while just to get back on their feet or reestablish themselves.

No matter how this current living condition came to be, trust me when I tell you that living with your parents is never a clever idea. (Even though this lesson deals with separating from thy mother and father, this also includes other family and friends.)

Just a quick side note: These arrangements are catastrophic to any marriage in any stage, but they are especially dangerous for newlyweds.

My wife and I have seen this on many separate occasions; one of you are okay with these arrangements, while the other is disgusted at the thought of it all. Don't get upset with your spouse if you're the one living in heaven with Momma picking up after you, cooking your dinner, and tucking you in at night. There is a reason they feel the way they feel; living with someone, no matter if it is your parents or not, it's not comfortable or God's plans for your marriage.

Let me stop. I know some of you are ready to move to the next lesson. You're thinking to yourself that this chapter does not apply to you and your marriage because you're not living with your parents. Let me tell you, just because you're living together physically doesn't mean you did not bring them in your marriage mentally. Not so fast, hang out. I am sure this lesson can help you as well.

Like I was saying, living with your parents was never God's plan for your marriage. Matt 19:4-6 says, 4 Jesus answered, *"Have you not read that from the beginning the Creator 'made them male and female' 5 and said, 'For this reason a man will leave his father and mother and be united to his wife, and the two will become one flesh'? So, they are no longer two, but one flesh. Therefore, what God has joined together, let man not separate."*

God stressed to us to separate from our fathers and mothers because he knew living with our parents, either physically or

Lesson 1

mentally, would disrupt some very important lessons we must learn for us to become one. Three lessons are:

- Learning How To Think Together
- Learning How To Struggle Together
- Learning How To Fight Together

I.   We must be able to think together

Once again, God gave us strict instructions to separate from our father and mother and become one flesh. This is especially true when it comes to thinking together as one. It's almost funny, but after almost seventeen years of marriage, my wife finishes my sentences. On many occasions, I will make a statement and she will quickly say, "I was just thinking the same thing." We think together, or alike. I assure you that this did not happen overnight. It has taken us years to come to a point where we think alike.

My wife is going to kill me for telling you this, but I can remember back about eighteen years ago, when I first came home to visit her prior to us getting married. Like I mentioned before, we were high school sweethearts, but due to unforeseen circumstances, we separated for about two years. During those two years, we were able to go out and experience all the people that were not for us.

During those two years, we encountered people emotionally, physically, and sexually. Without even knowing it, we had begun to collect pieces of the people we connected with, and we became like them in many ways because we began to think like the people we connected with. Once we came together sexually, we were so frustrated. The entire time we were together in school, we never had sex together.

(I know, that is amazing, right? But it wasn't due to the lack of trying. God just never allowed it to take place).

So, in our minds, we are thinking to ourselves that we were about to rock each other's worlds with all the lessons we have learned from other sex partners. Little did we know, this ended up being one of the worst sexual encounters of our lives. It almost ended our relationship before it got started again.

The reason it was so frustrating for the both of us was we had so many experiences in our heads that we were unable to experience each other; we wanted the other one to experience us and what we knew. That is almost the definition of rape. That is what happens when you first move in together; you immediately begin to force what you know and all your experiences on each other, causing things to be very frustrating at first. Therefore, you need to be as far as you can from each of your parents early on; being around them

Lesson 1

will make you comfortable with who you are, making it difficult for you to change.

I remember times when my wife and I would go visit her parents. As soon as we crossed her county line, it was like something came over her and her whole attitude changed. She would snap on me in front of her parents, talk crazy in front of her sisters, and dared me to say anything. This caused me to snap back, and to do that in front of her family caused World War III. We would be upset with each other for weeks at a time.

I must say, I was no better. When we would go around my family, my wife said that I would begin to be very controlling, and I would try to make it a point to show everyone I ran things. At the time, I did not notice it. I thought I was just being me, but that was just what I was doing: being the me I remembered when I was at home in my safe environment. This caused my wife to stand against me, causing me to get upset. It got to the point where we hated to go around our parents. We needed time to establish who we were without them.

We later learned that thinking together was a necessary evil for us to survive our marriage. After some time, we began to appreciate the purpose of thinking together. Doing so allowed us to understand one another, have an agreed upon approach, and support each other's decisions no matter what. Now, I need you to sit up in your seat and pay close attention to what I am about to teach you. This is one of the single most important lessons you will learn in this book. It is absolutely necessary that we learn to do each of these actions together as a married couple.

What you must understand is, thinking alike doesn't mean one partner has mind control of the other partner, or one partner doesn't have a mind of their own. Thinking alike means each person in the relationship understands how the other one thinks and feels about various things. This is a product of many days and nights of long conversations about each other's deep thoughts, sharing how you feel with each other and about issues you have faced or are facing. This is a product of allowing each other to have and express their feelings.

II. **We must be able to struggle together**

Another way parents gets in the way of a developing marriage is financially. In our journey to become one, we must learn how to win and lose together. In the next chapter, we will deal with how putting your assets together will help save your marriage. I must say, we would not have ever learned that valuable lesson if we continued to allow our parents to come between us and chime in on our financial struggles.

One day, I heard Bishop TD Jakes explain how baby eagles gain most of their strength from breaking out of their shell, and if

Lesson 1

their mother cracked the shell for them, they would not have the strength to survive on the outside. Therefore, the struggle of getting out was what made them strong. The same applies when it comes to your marriage; every time your parents help you out of a financial bind, it stunts your growth as a couple. The struggle is what makes you strong enough to survive on the outside of your parents' home. Struggling together financially builds dynamics.

1. ***Dynamics: a basic or dynamic force, especially one that motivates.***

Continuing to allow outside sources to interrupt your struggles also interrupts your ability to develop certain dynamic forces that will allow you to overcome stronger adversaries later in your marriage, such as budgeting, saving, and the ability to buy better things in the future.

The more we fought about money, lost utilities, and were limited by having a lack of money, the more we were forced to adapt and overcome. During our first fifteen years of marriage, all we fought about was money. Either I was controlling it, or she was wasting it. No matter what, money was an issue in my marriage but over the years, we became creative with ways to overcome our money problems. We were able to do so because there was no one there to help us out of the hole we were stuck in. We had to figure this out alone.

That is the best way to look at it. We were in a hole together; we could not leave each other. We had to figure it out or die there in that financial hole we had created together. Having a parent there would have allowed a way out for one of us, leaving the other one (to whom we vowed that we were there for better or worse) there to die alone.

Since we knew we were in this hole together, we fought each other, yelled at each other, we even tried to leave each other, but we were too broke to climb out. We started trying different options to get out. I would budget and pay bills for a while. She would budget and pay bills for a while. She would get a job so that she could help me out. I would rob Peter to pay Paul to make ends meet. No matter what, we went from fighting together to working together— until we came across one of the greatest programs in the world about five years ago: Financial Peace University, developed by Dave Ramsey. This program saved our marriage. We now understand that if our parents had continued to bail one or both of us out of our struggles, we would have never learned to survive together. We may have even given up being together due to becoming tired of struggling together. Struggling together financially builds dependency.

2. *Dependency: relying on someone or something else for aid, support, etc.*

Lesson 1

Struggling together did not only teach us the dynamics of survival; we also learned how to depend on one another. One of the greatest feelings in the world, as a married couple, is knowing that we're in this together; knowing that we are going to win together or lose together. Becoming dependent on one another causes us to push one another because when one win, we both win. If one loses, we both lose. One of you having that outside support takes away the motivation to need and motivate the other person.

Early on in our marriage, when my wife was not able to get her hair fixed, she would ask her father for help. Ladies, this is not a good thing, even though you're not allowing your parents to pull you out of a hole. In your mind, you're just getting something you want, but you're still violating your husband. In some cases, husbands do this as well. Your husband picked you up from your parents or asked your parents for your hand in marriage; when you go back to them and ask for money for things as simple as hair, clothes, shoes, or even a little throw away money, it makes him look as though he cannot take care of you. To you, it may seem so petty, but I promise you that this is a huge blow to his self-esteem.

The best thing you can do is let your husband know what you want, desire, and expect out of life. If you do this, not by tearing him down but by building him up, you will be surprised at the results you will receive from him. Even though my wife began to ask her father for things she desired out of habit, she quickly adjusted her actions once I informed her on how that made me feel.

Side note: It is important to share your feelings with each other and when you do, don't knock your spouse down for feeling that way. They can't help it; it is who they are. We will discuss this later in the book.

Back to what I was saying. Even though my wife did that in the beginning, she was also one of the greatest examples of how to build me up to give her what she needed, instead of tearing me down because I was unable meet her expectations.

Remember, you are two different people; what you know, your spouse does not know. What you like, your spouse may not like. When we first got married, I was used to living with the bare essentials of life. Let's just say I was po'; we could not afford the "o" and the "r" to say that we were poor. So, I did not want the greater things in life. I was very simple. My wife noticed this and, at first, she was not too happy about that. However, she exposed me to things a little at a time. After a while, I began to want the better things in life. It wasn't overnight, but it did happen. Women: remember your husband is what you make of him. Stop beating him down and build him up. Finally, struggling together builds determination.

3. *Determination - Firmly Decide*

Lesson 1

After years of struggling together, my wife and I finally concluded who we were and were not as a couple. Guess what? We learned that we didn't have to go to every Christmas dinner. On Christmas morning, we didn't have to respond to every call from Momma and Daddy, or other family as far as that is concerned. We were able to respond to the needs of each other, and not to the needs of those we were no longer responsible for. Let me tell you something: now that you're married, your number one responsibility is your spouse. Not your family; your family will cause you to get a divorce trying to continue to receive the luxuries you offered them prior to you getting married.

So, do not get into your relationship with all the predetermined conditions of things that you will and will not do.

1. I will not miss Christmas at my mother's house.
2. We will let our family move in if they need us.
3. I will give my family money if they need it.
4. I will not let you pull me away from my friends.

Statements like these put a strain on a relationship early on, creating boundaries that should never be established by one individual, but by both parties involved. Marriage involves two people, so both should have a say in all matters. It is a give and take relationship, and here is a bit of advice to help you decide on which things you should give in on, and which you should fight for: fight for the things that really matter to you, not your family. I am sure if your spouse loves you and you are willing to give in to the things that really matter to them, they will be willing to bend.

Once the two of you go back and forth for a while, determine what matters and what you may relinquish, you will slowly see your marriage transform into what the two of you determined it to be. Trust me, this is a lot more relaxing than the alternative. Granted, not everyone in the family will like it. They may even say that your spouse is running you and changing you. We heard these a million times but seventeen years later, we are still together and happily married, so it was worth it.

Your parents, whether they have survived their marriage or not, have had the chance to decide on who they are. It is your time to come to an understanding of who you and your spouse will be as one. Don't allow your family's past to dictate your future.

III. **We need to be able to fight together**

About fifteen years ago, I was sitting in my office at work, having what my wife and I like to call a heated fellowship. My supervisor was sitting in the office at the time. Once I got off the phone, he stated, "you and your wife argue quite a bit." I told him, "yes, we have our ups and downs." He laughed and made a very disturbing statement. He said, "my wife and I have been married for ten years, we have two daughters, and we have never had an

Lesson 1

argument." I looked at him with the most confused look that I could muster up. I was thinking to myself, *either he is lying, or somebody is hiding something.*

I'm sorry to say, but about five years later, they were divorced. Listen, as crazy as it sounds, arguing is healthy for any marriage. It would be nice to say that each person should be able to sit down like mature adults and come to a calm and well thought out conclusion without raising their voices. Unfortunately, that was not how my wife and I settled our differences. We argued. We are two different people, with two different backgrounds and two different expectations. That is why when my supervisor stated that he did not argue with his wife, I thought to myself that he was lying, or someone was hiding something. We argue to get what we want. If someone isn't arguing, chances are someone else is meeting the needs you're not. Be careful if they are smiling and you did not do anything to make them happy.

Like I was saying, my wife and I are two different people, and arguing was and still is a vital part of our relationship for us. Not that I am promoting arguing; I am just stating the facts. I don't want you to believe that just because your arguing, you're not meant to be married. However, I want you to understand two things about arguing with your spouse:

1. Over time, you should mature in your arguments.

2. There are rules you must follow.

Maturing in your arguments:

Even though I continue to express how common arguing can be, I want you to know that as time advances, you should mature in your arguments. They should become more strategic, planned out, and less aggressive.

My wife and I hosted a marriage conference in the first year of pastoring. We had an older couple to share some wisdom with us as well as those who attended. They shared a story with us about an eighty-year-old couple who had been married for over sixty years, and they looked just as in love as they would have on day one of their relationship. The lady telling the story said that she asked the couple how they remained so happy for so long. She shared with us that she was expecting this very long explanation from this little frail man, but all that he said was, "One fool at a time." He continued, "when she was a fool, I wasn't and when I was a fool, she wasn't."

All this very wise man was explaining was, we argued, but we matured over time and understood the power of timing. As we grew, we understood that arguing was not a time to win or lose. If you're one, you win when your spouse wins, and you lose when your spouse loses. Arguments are about getting the other person to understand how you feel. I will go into more details about this later in this book,

Lesson 1

but for now, I want you to understand that as time goes on and your love for each other grows, your arguments will be less about you winning and more about the marriage winning. You will care how each other feels during the argument.

Rules to fighting:

No matter how you were brought up, no matter how your mom and dad argued, you must follow the following rules to arguing.

1.   **No hitting**: I do not care what happens, you are to never lay hands on your spouse, unless you're loving on each other. This is an absolute deal breaker. I don't even care if they hit you. If you get hit, stop and separate from the situation as fast as you can. If you're still interested in your relationship after that, seek help for your marriage fast. Do not wait. That action came from deep down, and it will only get worse. Please listen to me on this and get some help.

2.   **No family**. The bible said, again, *separate from thy mother and father.* Listen: if you keep calling your family every time you get into it, you will be okay with your spouse at the Christmas dinner while everyone is still looking at them crazy. Secondly, if one or both of you has children from a prior relationship, do not allow them to get involved in your arguments. Stop that now. Even if they bring an

issue to you about your spouse, listen, but you are to never share your frustration about your spouse with a child.

3.   **No Red words**: No matter how mad you are, you can control what comes out of your mouth. Do not use any words that leave deep scars. The old saying is not true; words hurt more than sticks and stones. Sticks and stones bruise, and bruises heal. Words can cut you in places that can never heal. No cursing each other. You are adults; act like it, even in your disagreements.

4.   **No leaving each other**: Momma used to tell us, "you made the bed, lie in it." If you are woman or man enough to argue, you need to be woman and man enough to deal with it. I used to say don't go to bed mad. Well, that did not always work. I do stand firm in saying you're not allowed to leave. This is your relationship; deal with it. When you leave that house, you don't know what will happen. Don't give the devil an opportunity to come between you two.

As I mentioned in the beginning, I am noticing a lot of young couples living with their parents. This is so dangerous and unhealthy for your marriage. You need the space so that you can develop properly. God knew this was necessary; that is why He gave us the strong suggestions to separate from thy mother and father. That is the only way my wife and I survived our marriage. So, if you're in a

Lesson 1

situation where your family is in your marriage mentally or physically, I pray you have the strength to adjust.

Lesson 2
Putting Our Assets Together

Over the past seven years of pastoring and fifteen years of ministering, my wife and I have counseled many different couples. We can say that about ninety percent of the problems we encounter could have been avoided or detected a lot sooner if they would have had put their assets together. I know you don't quite understand that, but you will by the end of this section. I'm referring to issues such as infidelity, gambling, drug use, and sexual frustration. After long meetings with each of the couples, it seemed in nearly every instance that if they had combined their assets, they would have seen it coming, or the other person would have had a tougher time pursuing it.

You may not want to hear this again so soon, but God said come together and become one. I am here to tell you that if your assets are separate, you are not one. We tell people you already have a readymade divorce. If you decide to leave each other, all you must do is get your clothes, get your car, and move out of the house. My wife and I did not have this choice. We were too broke when we moved in together to have separate things, but I do believe this was God's choice for us. When we moved in together, I was living on a military base in Virginia, but all my assets were back home. I say all, like I had something. When my wife and I moved in together, this was the extent of the things we owned separately:

<u>My wife owned a</u>:

    I. bed

    II. dresser

<u>I owned</u>:

    1. Car

The funny thing is, when I started typing the list above, I thought we had more things beside our clothes and shoes, but no. That is all we had. We both had a job, but we did not have any savings, so we put her bed in our apartment, and I gave her my car to park outside. I must admit, the car was not that good, but that old Corolla lasted us a long time. God bless that Corolla. Also, I must say that it did not make much sense for us to use the words "my," or "mine," like so many couples do when they are not ready to merge together in the marriage. We did not have that much pride in the items we had.

We did not think much about it at the time, but as time went on, we looked back at our life and realized all the bullets we dodged by not having anything when we first got married and moved in.

Lesson 2

Can I pause for a second and speak to the men? I want you to know one thing. When I reunited with my wife, she was living with a friend. I visited her there, even slept there and slept with her there. I want you to know this: as soon as I married her, I went to the rental office for the same apartments and told them that I was heading back to Virginia, and my wife needed an apartment. Prior to me going back to my duty station, I made sure my duty back home was taken care of. Men, that is your wife; make sure you can take care of her prior to you taking her from her current conditions. That does not mean you must meet the standards of her prior living conditions, but you should be able to give her some sort of conditions she can live in. Prior to Adam receiving Eve as his wife in the bible, God made sure he had a job, a place to stay, and a relationship with God. So men, if you're going to marry her, make sure you at least provide her a place to live.

Back to the point I was making. We did not appreciate the struggle at the time. We just thought we had to figure out how to come up together. We did not realize, at the time, that we gained from quickly putting what we had together and becoming one as soon as we did in our marriage with our assets.

Gift 1: It's Harder to Separate

I mentioned earlier that people who live in the same house and do not put their assets together have a readymade divorce waiting to happen. We explain to couples now: your marriage should be like two pots of rice being mixed together. If you put your rice in a pot and she puts her rice in the same pot, it would be impossible to separate and see whose rice is whose. It would be easier to just stay together than to go through the hell of attempting to separate the assets. This is how you should want your marriage to be; so frustrating to separate that it would be easier just to stay together.

The first thing you need to do to mix your rice together is put your money in the same pot. Stop… stop… stop, stop getting in your thoughts of all the reasons this should not happen. I am here to tell you that the arguments you're avoiding are what you need to make your marriage stronger. I explained to you in the last chapter how arguments are necessary. So yes, you need to put your money together. Now, I know the frustration this will bring, but I am going to share with you a way that you can do this that, mitigate some of the aggravation, and allow yourself to put your rice in the same pot.

I will go into greater detail about this in the chapter titled, *"Romance without Finance is a Nuisance."* However, I suggest you first get three accounts. The first account will be a place where all the funds are deposited into, and I do mean all— even child support. There is no such thing as separate money; it all belongs to the house first. We will separate it later. This will be the general account where all the bills will be paid from. Once all the bills are paid, you should decide (together) what goes into the other two accounts.

Lesson 2

The second account needs to be an emergency fund. This will be where you keep money for that, and only that. The amount should be at least $2500. Finally, you should have a savings account where you save money for agreed upon reasons, such as Christmas, car, house, vacation, and any other thing you guys feel you should save money for throughout the year. Not only should you agree on the reason for saving, you should also agree on the amount and ensure that no one violates this account for other reasons without the approval of the other spouse.

You should always leave enough money to put in your pockets. This money is called *blow money*. This does not have to be a lot, because all the bills are covered, including food and gas. *Blow money* is money to do whatever you want; you choose, not your spouse.

I know that this is a lot to process, but we will go much deeper into this in the chapter titled *"Romance without Finance is a Nuisance."* The key things to keep in mind is you are now so invested together that it will be hard to leave each other. Not only will it be hard to separate the money, you also have a planned vacation, Christmas, and other family events that you have been working hard for. It will be disappointing to leave each other now over some small argument.

Gift 2: You're Stronger Together

The second gift we gained from putting our assets together early on in our marriage was learning that we were stronger together. The old saying is, "two heads are better than one." This also stands true when it comes to finances. Not that I am saying no one should be a housewife or house-husband. If this works for your family, so be it. My wife was a stay home mom 90% of our relationship, but if there are two incomes, it is easier to work them together versus working them separately.

I know some relationships that have their money separate; his money pays all the bills, and her money pays for all her desires. Other relationships split the bills and whatever they have remaining is their money. This works great, until one of them has financial problems and one of the utilities get cut off. Then, one of you blames the other, causing an unnecessary argument that could have been avoided.

This presents the first reason putting your assets together make you stronger. I told you earlier in the book that you are two different people. My wife and I like to say we're like zippers; where she's weak, I'm strong and where she's strong, I'm weak. We complement each other. I am the budgeter, and she is the spender. Early on in our marriage, we fought about this so much that we just knew we would get a divorce because of money. Once again, we were so broke when we got together that immediately, all our money

Lesson 2

was together, and we were too broke to leave or split it up. Therefore, we had to figure out how to make it work.

Later, we concluded that since I was so tight with managing our money, I would do better with budgeting our money. We also concluded that since she was great with spending the money, she would be great with buying clothes and planning vacations. Even though we came to these conclusions, that doesn't mean we agreed with actions right away; we still fought against each other's decisions because we are still two different people. Once again, fighting is not a terrible thing if you follow the rules; you mature and make each other better through fighting.

To ensure that your bills do not go lacking, you must learn to play to each other's strengths. I know it may be uncomfortable at first but be honest: you know your strengths and weaknesses. You know what you can and cannot do right now. Not saying you won't get better in the future but right now, you fall in one of two categories:

1. You're terrible at managing money, but you'd rather keep things the way they are so you can continue spending how you want and not have someone tell you what to do; knowing deep inside that is what you need, but too stubborn to admit it because you're grown now and refuse to go back to the way it was when you were living at home with mom and/or dad.

2. On the other hand, you know you are the one who should be budgeting but would rather not to keep peace. Ask yourself: are you really keeping peace or causing avoidable confusion? True, you are not arguing with someone who doesn't understand your true value, but you're going to go off as soon as something goes unpaid. You also must admit that there will be even more confusion in your heart when you learn you're the one who's going to have to pay the reconnect fees to pay for the point you were trying to prove.

The sooner you guys admit you guys are mentally stronger with your assets together than apart, the sooner many of those unnecessary arguments will be avoided. You will still get frustrated with each other, but it will be less unnecessary money spent on recovering from ego trips, and more spent on summer trips. You will get that one later. We agreed that I would do better at budgeting our money since I was so tight with spending, counted every penny, and was a better steward over what we had. I learned to allow her to plan vacations; she was more creative and cared more on the experience than on the cost. In the end, we were stronger together than separate. So, if you're allowing your spouse to cover bills and know they are not good with managing money, just so you can keep your extra spending money, you're wrong.

Not only are you guys stronger mentally with your assets together, you guys are also physically stronger with your assets

Lesson 2

together. *Together we stand, divided we fall* should be the motto for marriage. On many separate occasions, I see couples struggling separately, attempting to pay their own bills, buy their own cars, and take care of their own debt. News flash: when you got married, if each of you struggle separately, you will never be happy together. You did not get married to go through things alone; you got married to be a team. Stop being so stubborn that you cannot see the real need for total unity, from the bedroom to the bank account.

The bible teaches us that there is more power in two than one. We have no problem tending to each other's needs in the bedroom. When it comes to the bank accounts, we feel *"that's a problem you brought in the marriage, so that's not my responsibility or problem."* If you guys decide to put your income together, you can pay each of your bills, pay off your debt, and prepare for your future much faster. Working together to overcome financial burdens will be work, but in the famous words of Dave Ramsey, "Live like no one else, so that you can live like no one else." What he is saying is, go through some unpleasant things now that most people would avoid so that one day, you will be able to enjoy the wealth that most people only dream about.

Some spouses (but in most cases, the men) will tell the other, "baby, you spend all of your money on you, and I will take care of all of the bills and the food." This sounds good at first. I told my wife we would never use her money on bills. I never wanted to depend on her money. I wanted to be the man and handle everything. Either way, God did not design us to be separate. The bible says, "he is not the author of confusion, but of peace." He did not plan for either one on you to fall.

Gift 3: You Have Little Room for Dishonesty

When it comes to surviving your marriage, I feel as though this final gift is the most important of the three. One of the greatest offenses that invade our marriages and establishes grounds for divorce is deception. The moment trust is lost, it is nearly impossible to get it back.

The problem is, in most cases, the offenders really hate that they lost the trust, but their flesh was stronger than their intention. This is why it is so important that we do not set ourselves up for failure; some of us cannot be trusted with money. Okay, I thought we were being honest. See, the problem is you were not ready for a real marriage when you asked for or accepted the other person into your life.

When I got married, my wife knew I struggled with a very strong porn addiction. The bible says the truth shall set you free. It was something that I was introduced to as a little child, and I did not have control of it; it had control of me.

I want to stop here and tell each of you something. Addiction is a struggle that has control of a person. When you get married,

Lesson 2

don't think that just because you ignore addiction, it will go away. You cannot beat addiction because it controls you. If they tell you about their struggles, you are responsible to help them out. Now, if they refuse to accept the help needed, then I understand you not being able to be subjected to their lifestyle, but if they are trying, it is your responsibility to fight with them.

Back to the point I was making. I did not want this problem, but it was my reality. Therefore, to ensure this addiction did not destroy me or my marriage, I disclosed this to my wife prior to our wedding day. I did this to allow her to decide whether to sign up for the fight.

I have heard some people say you must keep some things to yourself. Well, I come to tell you that the things you keep to yourself, you will have to fight by yourself. If you tell your spouse, you can fight together. Today, my wife will still make sure some things don't show on television. She knows my thorns and my struggles. This is why it is important for us to put our money together; she is my accountability partner. She will notice if I get out of hand spending money on something that is not normal.

For some of you, the struggle may be with drugs, sex, alcohol, gambling, maybe even weight or health issues. No matter what, there is something you are addicted to that can cause harm to you and your relationship if you continue. You need to admit to yourself and your spouse: "I cannot be trusted with my own money." This will be the one of the hardest things you have ever done in your life, but I promise you that this will be the single most important thing you will do to save your marriage.

Trust me when I tell you that knowing someone is going to notice the money is gone makes you think twice. Even if you do make that mistake, they will catch it before it goes on too long. Listen, I know that these struggles are embarrassing, but if you can trust anyone, I promise you can trust your spouse. This is why it is so important to disclose these things early in the relationship. I will discuss this more in the chapter titled, "Let it all Hang out." They are there to help you; that is what marriage is all about. The more you trust them, the more they will trust you. Don't hold back now; it may cost you everything later.

Prior to getting married, you may have had it in your mind that there is no way you would ever put your money or assets together with theirs. Well, I pray something I have shared shed light on some existing or future problems you could face if your assets remain separate. Remember, marriage is not about choosing what you will join. Marriage is throwing it all together in one pot like the rice and figuring out how to deal with the things you don't like about each other later. Remember, marriage is work, but it's worth it. You're going to hear that quote throughout this entire book.

Lesson 2

Lesson 3
Christ is the Answer

You may or may have not noticed that I have not said much about God. I know I am a pastor and my wife is a first lady. I know that both of us were raised in church. When we got married, we were as far from church as we could be. I will never forget that when we told my mother-in-law we were going to get married, she suggested that we should sit down and receive counseling from her pastor and his wife. I may have considered it, but they suggested that we not even consider getting married until they prayed for days, weeks, months, or until they heard from God that we should or shouldn't get married. I remember thinking to myself, *"I am a grown man, I don't need anyone telling me when and if I should get married."* We ignored all advice anyone gave us about getting any type of premarital counseling. We thought we had it all figured out. Little did we know.

Ironically, as pastors now, my wife and I now marry people, and I refuse to marry anyone who refuses to receive premarital counseling due to the hell we went through our first five years of marriage. We went through capital HELLLLLLLLLLLLL. We now know a marriage with good spiritual counseling is not guaranteed to survive, but I can tell you that every couple that we married over the past seven years is still together. Counseling makes things much easier to face.

I know that the title of the chapter is *Christ is the Answer*, not *Counseling is the Answer*. In my book, they go hand in hand. The first question we ask couples in our marriage counseling is: have the two of you given you lives to Christ, or are the two of you saved? We ask this question for two reasons:

1. The bible says in Amos 3:3, *how can two walk together unless they agree*. We understand it is almost impossible for two people to live in the same house when one is saved and the other is not. We refuse to marry any couple that attends two different churches, has different religions, or where one believes in going to church and the other one doesn't.

We now understand why Amos wrote what he wrote in the 3rd chapter and the 3rd verse. Amos understood what we now understand; if two people begin a relationship with a disagreement as strong as religion, they are destined for failure. You are beginning a relationship where you will be forced to change who you are or go two separate directions on many different occasions, creating a gap that the enemy will use to destroy your relationship.

Lesson 3

I will never forget how my belief on this was challenged once. I thought about breaking the vow not to marry two people who had two different religious views a few years ago. My nephew was and still is very near and dear to my heart. He found the women of his dreams. To see them together was a very warm sight to witness. You can tell they were deeply in love; typical relationship with typical issues, but for the most part, they were in love. He jokingly asked me when they get married if I would consider doing the ceremony. I did not know how to respond. I knew he was a devout Christian, and she was a devout Muslim. I knew neither of the two was prepared to change. For a moment, I considered it for the sake of love, but quickly visualizing the reality of their two religious backgrounds, I had to quickly call my nephew and tell him, "I know you were just joking, but I highly suggest the two of you choose a religion to follow together prior to getting married, because it will be difficult for you to survive your marriage in the condition your relationship is in now." I hate to say it but a few years later, prior to the engagement or marriage, their relationship ended due to family religious views.

2. The second reason my wife and I do not marry couples without ensuring the two of them have given their lives to Christ is the reason we almost got a divorce in our first five years of marriage.

We learned early on that it was impossible to deal with some of the issues we had without the proper spiritual support.

I will never forget in roughly our 3rd year of marriage, I was sitting in the room with a guy who did not believe in God; his wife did not believe in God either. You could clearly see they had no spiritual boundaries. I began to ask myself, *"how can two people who honesty is limited to the sight of each other trust one another?"* I had finally reached a point where I appreciated the relationship my wife and I had with God. At that point, I was bound not only to please my wife in her sight, but to also please God in his sight. However, this relationship did not come easy.

Prior to us deciding to get back in church, like the both of us were raised to do, we faced a lot of issues that caused us both a lot of problems. Once again, these were issues I am sure a good marriage counselor would have picked up on and suggested we address prior to getting married. I never hit my wife, but I did put holes in walls, dents in cars, and broke things unnecessarily. To say the least, I had an anger issue; it was bad. I did not realize how bad it was. I used to drink to cover it up, but once I got married, I decided to quit drinking. Not knowing how to deal with the internal scars that created my anger issue, I took them out on my wife with words and actions.

Another sidebar moment: Ladies and gentlemen, let me tell you something. Just because you don't hit your spouse does not

Lesson 3

mean you're not abusing them. At times, this can be worse. Bruises heal, but words scar places that can never be repaired. We need to be careful with how we treat each other. Marriage is not a place where you discharge your frustration to hurt each other; marriage is a place where you discharge your frustration to restore one another. I know this may be confusing, but I want to stress that you should share your frustration for a very specific reason: to inform your spouse how to love you, not to hurt your spouse. I will explain this more in the chapter titled, *His Needs, Her needs*.

Being the woman, she was and having some issues of her own, my wife retaliated. She was not some pushover. My wife had a strong backbone. She would stand firm against me and do everything she could to get the worst part of me out. She would push me, talk crazy to me, and even stand flat footed and tell me to hit her if I wanted to. It would get bad. She had issues from her past that caused her to not respond well to someone trying to control her or talking crazy to her. We had some horrible word-lashing arguments.

It seemed as though who she was set me off, and who I was set her off. There were things I thought she should do and when she did not do them, I would get angry and attempt to push her to do them. When I pushed her, she pushed back, and the angry cycle started all over again. This went on and on for months.

Ironically, after we moved in together, we were in the middle of making love one day. We stopped in that moment where you're trying to decide if you're ready to get pregnant or not, and we prayed in the middle of everything and said, "God, if it is meant for us to have a baby, let it be; if not, God, block it. Even though we were not going to church, we still believed in God. It took us almost a year to get pregnant, because God knew no child should have been raised in that hostile environment. It was bad.

One day, I actually got so angry I grabbed my wife; today, she still says I shook her, but I say I just grabbed her. No matter what, I should have never touched her as angry as I was. She blew up and said to me, "Negro, I know you did not just put your hands on me." I was trying to get her to shut up and listen to what I was trying to explain, but that was the wrong thing to do. She took all her clothes and put them in a suitcase. She had her mind set on leaving me.

We were living in Mississippi at the time, over 360 miles from what we knew as home. The only problem she had with leaving me was that we were too broke to go anywhere, so I let her go. About ten minutes later, I went outside and could not find her. I later learned she was hiding behind a bush from me. She knew we had no money as well, so she called a cab and had him take her to the closest, cheapest hotel. She later answered her phone for me; I don't know why, but I thank God she did. I went to where she was. She suggested we stay there, but I asked her to please come home. I did

Lesson 3

not want to lay in a place that represented my wife leaving me. I wanted us to recover at our home.

Soon after that episode, we knew we needed a change. The frustration of our past problems clashing along our inability to conceive a baby put our marriage in a pretty bad place. We began, that day, looking for a church home. It was more than looking for a church home; it was us surrendering to God, letting him know that we were ready to follow the plan He had for our lives. I believe His will was in our hearts, but our desire to be free overshadowed His will for our marriage. We realized it was time to change when fighting to do what we desired almost cost us everything.

As soon as we began to follow the path that led us to Christ, it was as though the clouds left, the rain stopped, and the sun came out in our relationship. My God, just writing about it now is mind blowing. Listen to me: if you know God and you're refusing to follow what you know is right for your life, I promise you that nothing will go right for you until you do. My wife and I both had a call to serve God as children, and being so far from his will brought the worst out of the both of us.

As we continued to pursue a different direction for our lives, I felt as though something was working on the inside of me, changing me from the inside out. My wife changed as well, but at this point, I was no longer focused on God changing my spouse; it was more about God changing me. I felt like God put a mirror in front of my face, allowing me to see all the parts of me I did not like. I was not proud of the man I had become, angry and very inconsiderate of the people around me. I had built a wall that allowed me to maintain control of my environment so that no one else, not even my wife, could destroy my life again. If you did not fit my expectation, I would cause you to be very uncomfortable around me. I had allowed all the hurt and disappointment from my childhood to transform me into a bitter and angry person who had a low tolerance and a short fuse. I only noticed this when God began to show me, through His word, how I should be; I was far from it.

Like I was saying, I felt a change going on inside of me. This change took about eighteen months. I know it was eighteen months because it was so systematic; the journey was in six-month increments. Remember, in the first 6 months, God gave me peace. All the things I was angry about before did not matter so much. As I continued to go to church and seek to please God with my life, I focused less on my past and more on my future. I wanted to make my father in heaven happy with who I was as a man, and a husband.

Six months later, God touched my heart and along with the peace, he gave me understanding. Things I did not understand before were so clear to me. I realized every cause had an effect; nothing was by chance. I understood my wife and others around me, I was less angry because of the things they did, and I realized that hurt people

Lesson 3

hurt people. Instead of getting upset, I felt hurt for them. I realized they were only a product of their environment. It was not my job to add to their pain; it was my job to attempt to make their pain go away. I understood this because this is what God did for me. Even though I was this hurt, bitter guy, he still blessed me as I pursued to please him. He was a forgiving God, so how could I not forgive those who hurt me?

Six months later, one year from the beginning of this transformative journey, I soon learned I had control of nothing in my life, and I began to trust Him for everything. I understood I did not have control of anything, and that whatever God had for me was in His control. The only thing I could control was ensuring that I was where He wanted me to be when He wanted me to be there. It was around this same time that God blessed my wife to get pregnant with our first baby. This was the happiest, most exciting time of our lives. Our prayers were finally answered. It was as if God said we were finally ready to raise a child together now that we had begun to become one in Him, and not in us. That is what holds a marriage together: it's not the love you have for one another; it is the love you have for Him.

That is why I say Christ is the answer. He is the reason I became a better man, but most of all, He is the reason my marriage survived. I owe it to God to love my wife through whatever she goes through, and she must love me no matter what I go through. We do this because He loves us, and our marriage reflects the love He has for us. Therefore, we make sure couples understand why they say, "...to have and to hold, from this day forward, for better, for worse, for richer, for poorer, in **sickness** and in **health**, until death do us part."

You must understand that this is not just vow to each other; it is a vow to God. Because He loved us, we now vow to love each other no matter what. We will reflect his love through our relationship.

Lesson 4
Let It All Hang Out

Past, Present, Future

You know, the first thing that came to mind when I wrote this title down was an area that helped us survive our marriage: our up close and personal moments. Some of the coolest times my wife and I had during the earlier stages of our marriage were getting comfortable around each other. We are two different people. I am very open and straightforward, while she can be very shy and secretive at times. So, while getting up close and personal was a breeze to me, it was a bit of a challenge for her.

When I say up-close and personal, I mean stuff like being naked around each other, talking while we used the restroom, or even passing gas around each other. These were things I loved doing; it made me feel as though I was open with my wife. No one could say they experienced me like this but my wife. I was married, so it was time to let it all hang out. She took a little while to open up, but she eventually came around to some areas; other areas, she still has a problem with. Not me, though. I am cool with doing whatever around my wife; that is my girl. I'm not saying that since she is not cool with doing certain things around me, I'm not special to her; it just makes us different.

Side note: We must stop living our lives like much is given, much is required. One of the greatest mistakes I made early in my relationship was that I gave her what I wanted back in return; if she did not return the same action, I felt as though she did not love me. I later learned marriage is like the old barter system we learned about back in school. One farmer would trade his best for another farmer's best. One may have chickens, and the other may have cows. They would swap eggs for milk, meeting the other's needs. Not saying I gave you milk, so why did you not give me milk back? This is how marriages work; you meet each other's needs. We will discuss this more later in the book.

Even though I was comfortable being naked, using the restroom, and relieving gas around my wife, these did not save our marriage; they only made us closer. There was never a point where I felt as if we were going to get a divorce or separate because she would not talk to me while she was sitting on the toilet. There were areas in our lives that we did not share with one another, areas where we did not let it all hang out. We later learned that not sharing these internal issues with one another almost cost us our marriage on many separate occasions throughout our relationship.

Lesson 4

I need you to pay very close attention to the things I am about to share with you. These are possibly the second most important things that will save your marriage, the first being understanding that Christ is the answer. Now, you must let it all hang out.

At the beginning of our relationship, we suffered some intimacy issues. We discovered most of our intimacy issues resulted from our previous sexual encounters with other people. I explained earlier how we came together, after many years of not having sex, and our two different past experiences clashed. We were able to overcome that hurdle, and we began to enjoy our sex life. However, for me, something was still missing.

I was a touchy-feely guy. I wanted to kiss on my wife, hold her hand, touch her on her butt. I was very physical. That is how I expressed my emotions. For some reason, this was always an issue with my wife. She would never let me know why, but she would always say *stop, don't do that, not now, move*. I felt very rejected.

This carried on for years. At times, we would get into arguments. I would call her selfish, and she would say I was inconsiderate. In my head, these were actions that people who loved each other did to one another. I felt as though she did not love me. I was very confused and did not understand what was going on. There were certain things I would attempt to do while making love that she would not allow.

This continued for years, until we had an argument one day about that and some other things. During this argument, she finally shared with me that what happened to her as a child caused her to feel this way. I was totally surprised because I never knew that about her. Almost two years into the marriage, and she never let that hang out.

That day, we learned a valuable lesson and began to let it all hang out when referring to our past, and I do mean all. Many people do not believe this, but my wife and I have sat down on many different occasions and spilled our guts to one another about our pasts. I say on many different occasions because every time, we remember something we forgot to share. We do not have any secrets from each other. I know that is hard to believe, but I promise you we don't. If you're thinking to yourself, "you will never know what she never tells you," I guess you're right. I can only make sure I am honest. I always say that I am going to do everything on my end right, so if that day comes where she is living a lie, I will know I can leave with my head up knowing I did all I can do. You can't control the other person; all you can do is control you. I can tell you this, though: knowing you're not doing anything wrong is the greatest peace in the world. I always say I can't cheat on my wife because I would think to myself, *if I am able to do this and not tell, what can she do and not tell?* Therefore, I tell her everything so that I will have a free conscience.

Lesson 4

I know in your mind, you're thinking that they can't handle my past, and what they don't know won't hurt them. I promise you this: what they find out later will hurt both of you. Trust me, the devil doesn't play fair. As soon as you think you're finally happy and there is nothing that can get in the way of your perfect relationship, the devil will raise his ugly head up in the middle of everything. He doesn't want to see you happy. His entire plot is to kill, steal, and destroy. He will attempt to do so with your marriage by bringing up something from your past that you did not share, leaving you trying to salvage your relationship over something that could have been avoided by being open in the beginning.

The only weapon you have to fight the devil with is the truth. I always say, my version of the truth is much better than his version. One time, an ex-girlfriend approached me inappropriately while I was at work. She was very inappropriate with me. I first put her in her place, and then I ran upstairs to my office and told my wife exactly what happened. I did not want the enemy to use someone else to call her and give his version of the truth. I am a firm believer that the truth shall set you free. I believe once you have the truth, it is your choice to do with it as you please.

I know many of you are wondering what benefits I am gaining from opening up about my past to my spouse because right now, all you see this doing is creating confusion in my relationship. If you're already married and are trying to salvage an already rocky relationship, you might want to take it slow. If you guys have not been honest with one another, what you have not shared is the least of your worries; you should be more concerned about what they have not shared. You did not think about that, did you? You thought you were the only one who had dirt. Once again, that is why it is so important to start being honest as soon as possible, but go slow. Build up the tolerance. I highly suggest you sit down with a counselor during this process, someone who can help you guys through the journey.

If your marriage is rocky or if your just getting engaged, letting the past out early will allow you to have that peace I spoke of earlier. This peace will come because number one, you will not worry about anything popping up in the middle of your marriage, causing issues in the future. If it does become an issue, you will be able to say quickly, "I told you about this in the past, and I am not engaging in this any longer." Fortunately, your past is your past; we can't change our past, we can only make sure it does not affect our present or our future.

Now, on the other hand, you want to let someone know about what you have been through in your past, just in case you begin to struggle with this again. If your spouse knows your past, you can be more comfortable sharing with them what you are going through, and you won't feel obligated to keep it to yourself. The sooner you let your spouse know, the better, and you will be less

Lesson 4

likely to fall victim to the issue. Your spouse can also help you avoid situations that trigger your old problem.

When I got married to my wife, I had a bad addiction to pornography. I was always upfront about this. I was not hiding it; it was my problem. When I gave my life to Christ, this became an issue for me. I could not shake it. I spoke to my wife about my desire to stop, and she has been a great asset when it comes to me not falling back. I say has been, and not was because this is still a struggle for me. Seventeen years into our marriage, and she makes sure we don't watch some things on TV and when she goes to bed, she encourages me to come so that I will not be tempted. I have been going strong for about ten years, but without my wife's help, I would have never survived the fight against my fleshly desire.

I don't care what you have learned from your family about keeping some things to yourself; this is never a good idea. Ask yourself, *"how happy is their relationship?"* It is always easier to tell the truth than it is to cover it up. It always seems to surface. So, I challenge you to follow our example and let it all hang out. I love my wife more because of it, and most importantly, I do not want to leave her. She is the only other person who knows everything about me. I will never trust anyone as much as I trust her. We're Team Harden all the way.

Lesson 5
Serving the Right Way

Right after my first daughter was born, my wife and I were living the life. I had just been discharged from the Navy, where I served my country proudly. We had moved back to Houston, found a decent apartment, and God blessed us with a little girl. We were the proudest parents in the world. You could not touch our daughter unless you washed your hands and put on hand sanitizer. We had worked so hard to get pregnant, and we were going to make sure nothing happened to her.

Two days prior to her being born, God blessed me with an excellent job. It was temp to perm, but it was a good Job. I am proud to say that fifteen years later, I am still on that same Job. Having a child made me want to be the best dad I could be. My wife was an amazing mother; she was a natural. She put all that she had into being a mother, and I put all I had into being a father. We did not have much time for each other, but we did not complain much. We just understood that this was our new normal.

We knew when we came home, we had to find a church home. We did not rush at first, but we did not want things to go back to the way they were before. One day, we saw a family member of mine and she invited us to worship with her family at a church named Ebenezer Worship Center, under the leadership of Pastor Gregory T. Walters Sr. This ministry shifted our lives again. Now, we had a new baby, a new job, and a new church home.

We are not your normal church members; we jump right in and get to work. My wife immediately joined the choir and praise team. I later offered to record the services, and the pastor gladly accepted. Serving in the church was a great joy for both of us; it gave the two of us a sense of purpose outside of just what we did for each other. Serving God gave us individual purpose. Not long after being there, I finally accepted my call to the ministry. My wife was excited. I failed to mention that even though I went to church, it was hard dragging me there every Sunday, but the moment I accepted the call from God to preach, my whole life changed. I am now focused 100% on serving God.

Now, take a good look at our lives. From the outside looking in, we had it all together. We were twenty-two years old and living on our own with a brand-new baby. I had a good job, and we had two nice vehicles. My wife found a job by this time, and she was working. We were dedicated members of a church, where we both served faithfully. I was now a minister of the Gospel, preaching the word of

God to His people. I forgot to mention that I had become the youth pastor as well, causing me to spend a lot of extra time at the church and in my studies. We looked like the perfect couple.

Then, it happened. One day, I came home and was sitting in front of my computer, where I sat every evening after dinner to study the word of God. I would go to work every day, come home, and cook dinner; eat, and then sit down in front of my computer and study for a message I had to teach. Well, this day, my wife walks out of the bedroom, down the hall of our small apartment, and asked me this God awful, heart-wrenching question.

"Are you cheating on me?"

I almost blew a gasket. Actually, I think I did blow a gasket. I stood up and asked her, "What in the hell do you mean am I cheating on you?" Yeah, preacher and all cursing. I continued to say with frustration in my voice, feeling a bit neglected myself, "What make you think I am cheating on you? All I do is go to work, come home, cook, study the word of God, go to sleep, and wake up the next day to do it all over again. When do you think I have time to cheat on you?"

Then, she returned another heart wrenching statement; I knew when she said it that she had been thinking about it for a long time. She looked at me, never budging from her original position, and opened her mouth to say, "You're not talking to me, so you must be talking to someone else." After she made that statement, she walked off as if she just dropped the mic, and that is how I felt. I could not say anything. Life as I knew it just changed.

Let's back up for just one moment. Like I mentioned before, we had begun this new life. Serving God, working, new apartment, baby, and church was all good. However, you cannot take on all these new adventures that are very necessary and not make time for one another. God says to us that he will never put more on us than we can bear, but he never said he would stop us from doing so. We made some major moves in a short period of time, which affected our relationship in a major way. It was as if we both had created these two separated lives, and we were okay with it until my wife broke up our rhythm of madness with this legitimate question.

Now, let's look deeper into my situation. The reason I was so angry when she approached me with the question was because I thought I was the world's greatest husband. I later labeled myself as a textbook husband. I did everything the textbook would say a husband should do, and I was arrogant with it. I thought to myself, *"women you should feel lucky to have me."* Some women reading this book may even think you would love a man that did the things I did. That is because you don't know your worth. You're worth more than a man just doing what he is supposed to do. That was my job. I will come back to that in a moment, but I want you to know I was no angel.

Lesson 5

When she approached me with this question, I boldly got upset at first. I knew I had done no wrong and was ready to make her feel real stupid, until she redefined cheating right before my eyes. Up until that moment, in my opinion, cheating was a man putting his penis in another woman's vagina. My wife changed my life when she redefined it as conversation. I could have fallen to my knees and cried because I knew I was guilty. The man who vowed never to cheat on his wife, who bragged about not ever cheating and talked crazy to other men who cheated had now been guilty of the same offense.

With everything going on and all the changes in our lives, we had become very busy. I had become consumed with work and church, and my wife was consumed with work, church, and the baby. Without noticing it, we began to neglect one another, but we did not say anything; we just took it as our new normal life.

I. **The first lesson you need to gain here in this chapter is: don't just let things change without speaking up. Someone must break up the madness. I thank God my wife woke up.**

So, when I needed to talk, I did not disturb my wife with the things that were on my mind. I began to share them with another woman on my job. I did not think twice about it. I would go to her office every day, and we would talk about our lives. We would even discuss my wife and kids, her relationships, and her kids. It seemed normal, but I later learned that it wasn't. I became dependent on that conversation every day. Most importantly, I did not give this information to my wife. It was no different than me having sex with another woman, coming home, and my wife wanting to have sex, and me not having the desire because I had already emptied myself.

I later learned that I did not give my wife what she deserved. I had cheated on my wife, thinking I was serving her the way a husband was supposed to serve his wife. Unfortunately, I had shared something more precious than sex with another woman. I shared my dreams, vision, concerns, and desires with her through my conversation. Men and women listen to me: take my advice and don't do this. Women get pregnant with words, and they expect to give birth to the things you share with them. My wife deserved that conversation; she desired that more than me working, cooking, preaching, and having sex with her. She was disturbed because every night I came home after my daily routine, I would just go to bed and go to sleep. I had nothing to say during pillow talk because I had said it already to the other women. Writing about it now makes me feel even worse.

Ironically, God had me to preach a sermon about a similar scenario. It was about Mary and Martha, and how Mary served Jesus with all that she had, but Martha sat at Jesus' feet. Later, Martha became very aggravated with her sister and asked Jesus to send her sister to help her serve. Jesus replied to her, "...only one thing is needed and Mary has chosen that one thing, and it shall not depart

Lesson 5

from her." Jesus was telling Martha that serving just to be serving can all be in vain; it is better to sit down, talk to one another, and discuss the desire and concerns each of you have. Once you have that, you can then serve each other the right way. The right way is the way each of you need.

Later, in this book, we will discuss the importance of the needs of both man and woman in a marriage. We did not know about this until later in our marriage. For now, I will tell you to listen to your heart's desire. If you feel as though you're missing something in your relationship, speak up. Do not allow it to go on. Chances are, the other person in the relationship is missing something as well. It is your job to ask for it, and their job to deliver it. Don't allow your relationship to be destroyed by all the extra things you guys are doing. Always make time for one another.

Lesson 6
Staying Together No Matter What We Say

As I am writing this book, I am teaching you the lessons in the order that we learned them throughout our years of marriage. I don't know if you figured that pattern out or not, but I wanted to point that out to you. We learned this lesson around our fourth year of marriage. Thinking back on it, it feels as though we were married much longer than that. This was because we had gone through so much together by this time in our relationship.

I. We moved to another state, leaving our families behind to start a new life together.

II. We fought for a few years, trying to get to know each other outside of the high school couple we once were.

III. We suffered through almost a year of not being able to have a child. That was so heartbreaking, but God knew what was best

IV. We found ourselves spiritually, joined a local church, and began to serve God with our lives the way he desired us to.

V.   We moved back to Texas, found a new church home, I became a minister, and my wife found a new job, then God blessed us with our first baby.

Wow, all of this in our first four years of marriage. Now, this lesson finds us living together in our fourth year of marriage in our fourth apartment, and now with our second child. Yep, God blessed us with another baby girl. We were doing pretty good financially for the first time ever. God was really blessing our family with favor in so many ways. We were starting to mature and realize that we were a family for real.

During this year, we took our first vacation. One day, we woke up and said *let's take a trip;* we did not have the money but wanted to do something different. This was one of the greatest and dumbest things we had ever done. It was the greatest moment because it was the time we began making our first happy family memories. We still look back on those photos.

Sidebar: It is vitally important that you plan trips together as a family. No matter how much you work or how much you must do, a family that doesn't play together is missing one of the greatest experiences as a family. You will never witness your family at the level of happiness that a family trip puts your family on. Your family turns into an entirely different family. Don't rob yourself or your family of this opportunity.

Lesson 6

It was the dumbest because we did not plan it, and we really did not have the money. Ignorantly, we decided to allow the cable, phone, and other bills to get behind to justify us going on the trip. We eventually got caught up, but not without some unnecessary pains such as our lights being disconnected. That was not very funny, but we did laugh about it together. We survived, but I do not recommend allowing your utilities to suffer to justify a vacation, but I do recommend taking a family trip.

During year four, we also relocated to another ministry that really focused on faith, fellowship, and family. You could see that the pastor truly loved his wife, and we had never witnessed a relationship like theirs. The way he loved on his wife and the way she loved on him were very healthy for our relationship. We learned so much being around these two and the people in their ministry.

Another sidebar moment: Make sure the ministry you attend promotes a healthy lifestyle for your marriage. I never thought of this before, but it was one of the factors that helped us survive our marriage.

Even though we were living the life and enjoying each other so much more, each of us still had residue from our pasts on the inside. Let me tell you something: you will not get over who you are overnight. I tell my wife all the time that it took me twenty years before we got married to become who I was, so it is going to take at least that long or more for me to change. We have been married seventeen years at the time of me writing this book, and I am better than what I used to be, but I still have some of my old controlling ways.

Yes, I was still very controlling, and she was still very stubborn, causing us to have some pretty bad arguments at times. Every now and then, these arguments would lead to us doing something that was not healthy at all. At times, if the argument reached a point where one of us felt overwhelmed, one of us would leave to get away. Sometimes, one of us would pack our bags and pretend to leave the other one. I say pretend because we never went anywhere; we just packed our bags for nothing, just putting on a big show. We never left overnight, but we would leave the house for long periods of times.

I do not recommend this to anyone; stepping away, going into another room maybe, but leaving is not the answer. I strongly discourage you from going and staying over with a friend, family, or even a hotel. I told you earlier, you do not want to give the enemy the opportunity to come between you and your spouse. He doesn't play fair; that will be the time his or her ex will call, or a message will come across Facebook from an old friend. This is not the time to leave each other; you need to stay and face the storm you helped create. If you feel as though you can't handle being around your spouse during arguments for safety concerns, you need to seek

Lesson 6

professional help from a counselor or an anger therapist. This is your partner; you should be able to hash things out together without the fear of your spouse leaving.

One day, my wife and I had a very intense argument. I cannot remember what we were arguing about, but I can almost guarantee you that it was about me controlling our money. That was the root of most of our arguments: money. We argued about money because she wanted to be grown and spend what and when she wanted, and I wanted to tell her when and what to spend it on.

No matter why we were arguing, the point is we were arguing. Most of the time, I would be the one who would leave the house in the middle of an argument. I thought it would make her worried that I would not return and cause her to call me apologizing. That never happened, no matter how long I stayed gone. When she did not call, I became even angrier. Other times, it was her who would leave; she would pack her bags and walk out the door, as if she was leaving me and the kids. I don't know how many times I had to go outside, get bags, and bring them back upstairs to our apartment. This was an ongoing cycle. We would say things to each other like...

I. I would rather you be happy without me than be unhappy with me.

II. I am going to just leave to make you happy.

III.   I am not the one for you; if I was, you wouldn't be upset all the time.

IV.   You will be better off without me.

Each of these statements was an attempt to do the same thing us leaving was trying to do: deflect the situation on the other person. Make them feel as guilty as possible in order to gain leverage in the argument.

Much like many of our arguments, things got heated and this time, she just got fed up and walked out of the door. She said that she could not take it anymore and just left. We had done this to each other so much, until we could not tell if our marriage was over or not. It was toxic to our relationship and our kids. They watched us go through this on many different occasions. I don't care how old they are, they know something is not right with momma and daddy.

My wife left me sitting there in our living room angry, confused, and frustrated. Once again, I did not know if this was the last time I would see her or not. She did eventually return, but I cannot tell you how long it took; it felt like hours. I did not know what to think. This was not like her. I now knew how she felt when I left; it was the worst feeling in the world. I felt like she walked away from her family, her responsibilities, and her marriage. I knew, at that moment, no one should ever feel as though an argument would push the very person they love away.

Lesson 6

When she returned, I was sitting in the living room waiting for her. She walked in with her "I don't care" look on her face. I interrupted her with the most humbling voice I could muster up. I knew if I said the wrong thing in that moment, the conversation would have been over before it started. So, I humbly said to her, "baby, can we talk?" It was as if she was thinking the same thing; we both knew that this threatening to leave each other had to stop. When she sat down, I told her how much I loved her, and how sorry I was for hurting and upsetting her. I explained to her that I never meant to hurt her in any way.

I continued with this question: "Baby, do you love me?"

She replied with sarcasm in her voice, "Clyde, you know I love you." I must say that it was a relief to hear.

I continued, "I want you to know I love you as well, but while you were gone, I realized something: we need to promise each other that we will never leave each other." I continued by telling her, "As I sat here tonight, I realized every time we get into an argument, one of us leaves, causing the other to wonder if the relationship is over or not, and I understand after tonight how unhealthy this is for our marriage."

She listened to my heart that night like she never had before, and I concluded my request to her that night by asking her this question: "Can we tell each other tonight, unless there is infidelity or abuse, we will not leave each other, no matter what we say or do?"

She looked at me and said, "I agree, but you must agree to do the same." She looked at me with concern in her eyes and continued to say, "You make me feel the same way when you leave. I never know if you are coming back home when you walk out that door. So, you must make the same promise."

I looked her directly in her eyes and said, "I promise."

I know many of you are thinking to yourselves that it is better for me to leave than to go off and say something to hurt your spouse more. You're wrong; fighting shows that you love each other enough to get through the issues. Leaving says you don't have the energy to deal with the person you're arguing with. I did not realize that lesson until that day. That person is sitting there wondering if you will ever come back, or if they will be left to raise those kids alone. The things that run through your head during this time are horrible. They're thinking to themselves, *"if you have a wreck and die while you're out, the last conversation the two of you had was an argument."* They're also thinking to themselves that you're out with another person. If you love this person, you should never want them to suffer this way. If you feel as though their actions are making you suffer, go get help. No matter what, you should never walk away.

Lesson 6

In your mind, you think you're fixing the issue because when you leave and come back, the arguments become less and less frequent. It feels as though they are learning their lesson. Well, you are right about that; they are learning a lesson. The lesson they are learning is, they are not allowed to have feelings and share them with you. They are not allowed to get upset with you and tell you what they are thinking. So, this person you love ends up becoming very numb, needing so much, but keeping a closed mouth to keep a happy marriage. What you are creating is a ticking time bomb. I always tell people you never worry if a spouse is arguing with you; that means they think there is still hope for change. You should get worried with a spouse who doesn't say a word; that means they have given up.

You don't even realize what you're doing. Yes, the vocal lashings they once shared may have subsided, but you will also lose intimacy, compassion, and the love they once had for you. It is hard to love someone you can't share your feelings with. So many of us are so confused when it comes to understanding love. Love is when you care for each other more than you care for yourselves. You love yourself by taking care of each other's needs prior to your own needs. Therefore, how can you love your spouse the way they need to be loved when the result of them sharing a problem or issue with you is your walking out on them?

What will happen is your spouse will end up keeping all their desires inside and only take what is given to them, leaving them feeling empty on the inside. That is how I was making my wife feel every time I walked out on her. I know this because that was how I felt when she walked out on me. I knew, in that moment of sitting there in our two-bedroom apartment and waiting for her to return, we had to make a change. This could not be the way our arguments ended. We had to make a change.

I guarantee you that this will not be an easy process at all. Everything will push you to return to your old habits, but when you get ready to walk away, you must tell yourself that if you do, you will be opening the door for your spouse to do the same thing to you. You must be willing to make a huge sacrifice to avoid this vicious cycle from starting all over again. It will be tough, but I promise you that the security of knowing your spouse is in the this, for real, for better or worse is worth all the effort you put into making sure you hold up your end of the deal.

So, I challenge you— yes, you— to sit down with your spouse and clear the air in your relationship. Tell her or him, "no matter what we argue about, as long as there is not physical/mental abuse or infidelity, we will not separate under any circumstances. We are in it to win it." I promise, if you two do this, you will be one step closer to surviving your marriage.

Lesson 7
Its Too Late They Already Feel It!

I learned many lessons over the years about the do's and don'ts of marriage, but I must say this lesson has not only made an impact on my marriage, but also a major impact on my life. I learned this lesson during one of our Sunday evening group dinners. A group of us would get together and have dinner every Sunday after our church service. We gathered with about two other couples every Sunday evening after service; each couple would cook a dish, then we'd all come together and talk about so many different things. We would discuss church, current events, family issues, relationship struggles, and much more. It was during these meetings where I first started ministering to people.

These meetings were very therapeutic at times; on many occasions, these meetings took a turn for the worst. We would all get into a deep conversation, and someone would say something that would offend their spouse. Sometimes, the offended spouse would show their frustrations, but they would not say anything. However, we all knew that when they got in the car, it was going to be on and popping. Issues like this were all fun and games— until you were the one that was going to have trouble on the way home.

On many occasions, we were that couple with the problem on the way home. It never failed. I would get to speaking my mind, and I would end up saying something that offended my wife. I would know the exact moment when her attitude changed; I also knew I was in for a long ride home. From that moment, I began to dread the drive home, and we both would get quiet for the remainder of the time with the other couples. Everyone would notice that I was in trouble. My wife was, and still is, easily embarrassed, so it was nothing for me to say something that I should have kept to myself.

So, here it was. We left the house, and everyone gave us a hug goodbye. We got in the car, and there was dead silence. I went as long as I could without saying something, but when I could take it no longer, I asked her, "What did I do?" I cannot remember what it was exactly, but I do know It was something she thought was wrong, and it upset her. I went to explain to her how she took it wrong, how I did not mean it the way she took it, and how she blew everything out of proportion. I later learned that I wanted her to tell me what she was upset about so that I could defend myself and tell her how wrong she was for feeling the way she felt. However, my wife said something this day that blew my mind, and hers as well, when I

Lesson 7

brought it to her attention. In the middle of our argument, she told me, "Clyde, you can't tell me how to feel."

I realized, at that moment, I was arguing with her with the intention of changing something I could never change: how she felt right then. It was too late; she already felt it. I could not turn back the hands of time and fix how she felt. Let me explain: my wife was offended by something I said. In that moment, she felt a certain emotion that was generated by my actions. Let's look at this from another angle:

1. If I hit my wife and she said I hurt her, there is nothing I can do to take the pain away from that moment. All I can do is make sure I never do to her what caused that pain.

2. What we end up doing is measuring what we can take, then put that expectation on people. When they can't take what we can, we say that they are sensitive, and they are overdoing it.

3. We then go into a full-on debate, trying to inflict our ideas of what should and should not hurt, offend, frustrate, or even upset another person.

I learned that day that my wife was not me, and I was not my wife. She felt what she felt, and I felt what I felt. Once she came to me and shared how she felt, there should have never been an argument. I should have only said, "Thank you for letting me know how I made you feel. I promise that I will do my best to never make you feel that way again." Instead of doing this, I wanted to ignore how she felt and control her mind to believe the way I believed. Now, that is mental abuse, but I did not know it at the time. I thought I was only trying to share with her what I was really doing versus what she thought I was doing. However, when I told her that she was wrong for feeling that way, what I was really telling her was, "When I do what I did to you, I expect you to think and feel this way. Don't feel the way you feel or think the way you think, and don't you dare get upset with me when I do this in the future." I know I was controlling and running my wife crazy, and I did not understand why she was so frustrated with me.

My goal was to do something that was impossible: I wanted her to change the way she felt in that moment. So many of us are arguing to change how someone feels in a given moment; unfortunately, you cannot. That is impossible. All we can do is accept how they felt, and do our best to make sure they never feel that way ever again. I know this is not as easy as it sounds for many of us because it goes against everything we have learned our entire lives. Many of us was trained to defend ourselves against all odds; in order to win a fight, the other person must lose. Well, that works for wrestling, boxing, and other combating situations. It does not help in any partnership or relationship. Whether you believe it or not, marriage is a partnership. The best way I can describe this partnership is by comparing it to a three-legged race. If you plan to

Lesson 7

win this three-legged race called marriage, you must change your understanding of what it takes to win.

Understanding Change 1:

No longer do the rules say, *one will win and one will lose.* The rules now say, *in order to win, you must learn how to work together.* When we are in a fist to fist combat situation, most of us are not thinking to ourselves, "I wonder how the other person feels when I am hitting him." Most of us are just trying to win by any means necessary. That is because when you win, they lose and when you lose, they win. So, it's no holds barred. You will do whatever it takes to win.

Well, the three-legged race called marriage is not won this way. If you plan to win this three-legged race, you must care about the other person. If your partner quits and gives up, you lose as well. If they say they cannot take what you're doing to them, you must choose to change or drag them. Dragging the person represents the fights each of you have along your journey together. If you don't change, you will end up fighting and not advancing, fighting over stuff that could be adjusted a little for the marriage to advance. Instead of advancing and winning the war of marriage together, we would rather stop and fight for one of us to win a small battle.

If you plan to win and survive your marriage, it is in your best interest to learn how to listen to your partner when they say what they can and can't take. Now, a good team does not accept defeat due to their inabilities as individual teammates. A good team works together and learns how to compensate for the other's disabilities, until that disability becomes an ability. The word of the day here is *compromise.* You must decide that you will do what your spouse can't do, but you will also work with your spouse until they can do it.

There is so much I need to share with you here. We don't just stop and *say she can't do that, he can't do that.* We work together and help each other out. *You don't clean, I will clean; you don't cook, I will cook.* My wife and I call it the *Zipper Effect.* Where she is weak, I am strong; where she is strong, I am weak. We work together as one team and strengthen each other, but we don't allow each other to stay weak. We work to build each other's weakness so that we will be even stronger together. We will discuss this in more detail in the final chapter of this book.

The moral to the story is this: in order to win this race, you must understand that when your spouse says they feel as though they cannot do something, it is not your job to fight with them; it's your job to work with them.

Understanding Change 2:

When your spouse comes and explains that something you're doing is hurting them, they are not trying to attack or hurt you; they

Lesson 7

are trying to protect and help the marriage. You are one, running a race together. Therefore, if one of you is hurting, the other one is hurting as well. Ask yourself this: why should you fight when the other person says *you hurt me when you did this or that*? Like I explained earlier, I took it personal when my wife said I hurt her when I said what I said. I was so headstrong on changing how she felt instead of just changing what I'd done.

Many of us were raised to believe that you should not allow your spouse to change you. You must stay who you are and if you change, they are controlling you. Well, I say the opposite; if you don't change, you're trying to control the other person. You're trying to change how they feel. Your job is not to change how they feel, but to change how you made them feel. If that means you must change something you are in accustomed to doing, so be it.

Now, don't confuse this with changing your physical appearance to please someone. Your physical appearance and physical actions are different. It is love that causes us to change our physical actions to make someone comfortable in a relationship; such as, how we speak, handle, treat, or even make love to each other.

Side note: Yes, I said make love. My wife always asks for me to change this and change that to increase her joy in our sex life. I will make the same request as well. We do this because we want each other to equally enjoy it. I make requests as well. I always say that what makes me different than another man is I know exactly what my wife wants and needs to make her happy. I listen to whatever she asks and do it gladly.

Back to what I was saying. It is love that make us change our actions to make our spouse happy, but it is fear that causes us to change our physical appearance to make our spouse happy in a relationship. One may be afraid that their spouse will find someone who looks the way he or she wants them to look, or one may be afraid their spouse will leave if they do not meet the physical expectations their spouse has for them. Either way, pushing someone to change their physical appearance for selfish reasons is not at all what I mean when I say *change to make your spouse happy*. Changing for health reason is one thing; being selfish is something entirely different.

Now that we have that cleared up, I want you to know that if your spouse asks you to change your actions to allow them to be more comfortable in this race with you, don't take it personal. Take it as them giving you instructions on how to love them and make them happy in the relationship. If you listen, you will not only have a happy spouse, but a happy marriage as well.

Understanding Change 3:

Lesson 7

Amos 3:3 says, "Can two people walk together without agreeing on the direction?"

Most arguments happen in a marriage because of the lack of planning. What happens is, one of you will make a move without consulting the other person, only to find out that the partner was not happy with the decision. Remember, you two are tied together so when you tried to make a turn, they had planned to go in the opposite direction. Now, you end up with this dilemma: do you come back and go their direction, or do they decide to follow your move? This scenario usually ends after a very intense argument; either one party concedes, or you both end up just staying where you started with no advancement at all.

Situations similar to this are how most relationships end up very unhappy. They end up stuck, or just going in the direction of the most dominant partner. This is a divorce waiting to happen. My best advice for you is to follow the advice offered in Amos 3:3. Amos asked the loaded sarcastic question, "How can two walk together unless they agree?" I say sarcastic because he knew the answer before he asked the question. He knew that the answer was, they can't. Therefore, the only solution to this problem is planning your next move. I always say, people don't plan to fail; they just fail to plan.

The best way to ensure that you guys advance to an agreed upon level is to come to an agreement. Once again, you must be willing to accept their feelings of why they do, don't, can, and can't do what your suggesting. We learned earlier on that it's better to argue before we go, then to argue along the way. Sit down and go over the plan with open hearts, caring about each other's needs and not just your own. Come to a conclusion that best fits the marriage, not you as individuals, and you will see your marriage advance in ways you never seen before.

You must remember that marriage is a team sport. It is won or lost as a team. You can't say it was *his* fault or *her* fault. It was the team. With this in mind, you must remember it is in your best interest to get up and fight together as a team for the marriage, and not against each other in the marriage. Also, remember that no matter what you think, you cannot change how they feel; it's too late, they already feel that way. All you can do is make sure you don't make them feel that way again.

Lesson 8
Truth Moment!

Around year five, my wife and I began to watch different television shows together as a couple. This was one of our family pastimes. She would watch football with me, and I would watch Lifetime with her. Those were the days; we just enjoyed spending time together. She became my best friend all over again, much like we were back in high school. At one point, our favorite show to watch together was, *The Game*. This was a primetime show that aired on a TV station known as *The CW*. It was an amazing show the we absolutely fell in love with. It had the drama my wife loved, and football that I loved— the perfect marriage of entertainment!

We not only fell in love with the show, but with the show's power couple, Derwin Davis (played by Marion H. Hall Jr.) and Melanie Barnett (played by Tia Dashon Mowry-Hardrict). In the midst of all the dramatic issues the show had to offer, this couple stood out as a positive example. They were a great example for my wife and I during this time in our marriage, and their relationship reminded us of ourselves in so many ways:

- They were young, as were we
- Melanie had put her career on hold to support Derwin in his pursuit of his dreams, just as my wife had done when she left her job to support me in the pursuit of my dreams.
- They were both trying to please God with their actions, much like my wife and I were doing as well

There were so many similarities between our relationships that it is hard for me to list them all. During this time, my wife and I had a great relationship, but we would still argue all the time. Every time we tried to discuss an issue we had with one another, it would always turn into a debate or argument. We had become very defensive in this stage of our relationship. Even though we had just learned the importance of hearing each other out, it was still difficult hearing someone attack our intentions without defending ourselves. If we planned to survive our marriage, we needed more. We needed a way to communicate our needs, concerns, and problems in a way the other person had to listen without arguing back. Amazingly, my wife did just that and found a way for us to share our heart's desire, frustrations, and concerns with one another without the other

Lesson 8

person talking back at all. This was simply amazing, if I must say so myself.

I made it home from work one day, and my wife had re-watched an episode of *The Game* that we'd previously watched a few nights before. She explained to me how Derwin needed to say something to Melanie that he knew was going to upset her, but prior to saying it to her, he asked her this question: "Can we have a truth moment?" Once he said this to her, he also reminded her that she could not say anything back during this time; she could only accept what he had to say. She had to also promise not to get mad.

My wife doesn't come up with many suggestions like this; if we began to argue, she would usually just shut down and not say anything at all. My wife hates confrontation, so her coming to me making this suggestion made me feel as though she thought our communication had fallen off, and we needed to repair it. Hearing her heart's request, I gladly agreed. At that moment, I did not realize how much that decision would change our lives forever. The decision to follow my wife's suggestion not only blessed our lives, but also the lives of the couples we taught how to use it. We hear couples all around us saying to each other, "We need a truth moment."

This was the answer to our prayers; a way for us to let each other know what was on our hearts without all the backlash. We both concluded that we would use the words *truth moment* whenever we had something to share with one another that was near and dear to our hearts— without any debate and anger. We had to agree not to get mad or respond in any way. A truth moment will never work if you get quiet, frustrated, and walk away upset. The person will then revert back to keeping everything on the inside. The only response we can give at the conclusion of a truth moment is, "I accept what you have shared with me, and I promise I will do my best to comply with what you have asked of me."

I promise you, these two words changed our lives. Twelve years later, we still use this concept faithfully. We no longer call it a *truth moment*; we have a new secret word for it now that I cannot share with you. We had to change the name because we had taught so many people how to use *truth moments* that people began to use the phrase with everyone. One day, another woman from the church walked up to me and wanted to share something with me that was on her mind, and she asked me for a truth moment. I felt violated. That was my wife's word for me, and no other woman should have felt as though it was okay to put me in a place where I had to listen to her. She did not realize what she did; to her, she was only asking a question. To me she, was putting me in a place to care about her needs and surrender to her every word. In that moment, those words were no longer sacred. I immediately went home and changed our two words. My wife and I vowed to each other, that day, that we

Lesson 8

would forever teach couples to have truth moments with one another, but we would never share our new words with anyone.

I challenge you to create a word system only you and your wife know, one no one else can violate. Remember, when you use these words, it is as though you're asking your spouse to get naked, and you never want anyone to know how to get your spouse in that kind of vulnerable position. This is a sacred moment between you and your spouse, and I challenge you to keep it that way.

If used properly, this system will change your marriage forever. So go now, tell your spouse that it is time for the two of you to learn how to communicate your feelings with each other without the consequences of getting into an argument. Tell them you have learned a new way to share your feelings without the repercussions of getting into a fight after words. Develop your own truth moment, or should I say moment of truth. I pray this helps your marriage as much as it has helped mine.

Lesson 9
Romance, Without Finance, Is A Nuisance!

Looking back over the years of our marriage, I have to admit that money was the one thing we argued about the most. Seventeen years later, we are much better than we once were, but we still have our issues every now and then.

Side note: If there is one thing I want you to get in your head while reading this book, it is that no matter how long you're married, you will always have issues pop back up. No matter if it was year one, seven, or seventeen, we have issues with money and other things. Surviving your marriage is not about getting rid of all the problems in your relationship; it is about learning how to manage the problems better in your relationship.

There were three main reasons we fought about money, and I am willing to bet that there are three main reason each of you fight about money:

1. We did not have enough of it
2. I was very controlling with the money
3. In my eyes, my wife was very careless with the money. (She may define it different in her book, but this is my book... LOL)

I know some marriages have lots of money; that was not the case in our relationship, but some couples may have this luxury. Even though they have money, number two & three seem to be the case in every relationship. In most marriages, one person is conservative with spending money while the other is liberal. Whether you are broke or wealthy, I am sure this chapter will be a blessing to your life. For those who are familiar with the money struggle, we learned early on that romance without finance is a nuisance.

Even though wealthy people still have problems with money, I am sure it is not the top problem on their list. I'm sure money falls below other things, like compassion, communication, and intimacy. Many couples with money say they would rather have these items in place of money. On the other hand, when you're broke, the lack of money gets in the way of compassion, communication, and intimacy. It is very difficult to lay down and make passionate love to one another, knowing that the lights have been disconnected. No lights, water, phone, or cable just kill the entire mood of love making and passionate communication. Candlelight should be an option, not a necessity.

Lesson 9

Most arguments, in moneyless relationships, usually stem from the reason for the lack of money. Like I mentioned before, I was raised very conservative. I had no problem with having few material items in the house and having lots of money in the bank. I was raised with a black and white pantry. Everything we bought was black and white; *Better Value*. Most young people today are not familiar with Better Value. All Better Value products came in black and white packages. Being raised this way, I was okay with having little to nothing in the cabinets, paying the bills late, and even having services interrupted, even if we had money in the bank.

My wife, on the other hand, was raised more liberal than I was. She may argue with this, but once again, this is my book. To get her point of view, you can feel free to read her copy. When I say she was much more privileged than I was, I mean she was raised with a colorful pantry. Her mom bought things that had different names, such as Borden Milk, Heinz Ketchup, and Mrs. Baird's Bread. Her biggest struggle was choosing which box of cereal to eat from, not if they had enough milk to even eat the cereal. She did not understand empty pantries, paying bills late, or interrupted services.

Our diverse backgrounds caused problems in our marriage. We did not know how to get around this dysfunction early on in our relationship. We thought our marriage was doomed and destined to fail. We argued at least once a week about money. I would have, in my mind, how the money was going to be spent. I had everything budgeted in my mind, all the way down to our last dime. Out of nowhere and without informing me, my wife would go and buy McDonald's, messing everything up. I would be furious— how could see spend money without telling me?

No matter how much money we had, to ask me to spend money made her feel like a child all over again. In her mind, she had worked hard to be liberated from her mom, so she was not about to walk into another situation where she had to ask for anything. She knew how much money we had just like I did. She had planned, in her mind, what the money was going to be used on, just like I did. We just had two different perspectives on priorities. In my mind, my priorities were more important and, in her mind, her priorities were more important.

I was so controlling that I refused to allow her to get a Job. Don't judge me! I thought I was being "the man." I thought it was my job to go to work, pay the bills, and allow my wife the opportunity to relax at home and not worry about anything. Little did I know, I was only giving her everything she wanted to be able to put limits on her. Once again, I was only controlling everything. Men and women, be careful with this mentality. This is a "much is given, much is required" mentality. In our minds, we think that if we give-give-give-give, then a person should do whatever we ask. We truly believe that this is the least a person should do. This is controlling behavior at its worst.

Lesson 9

To avoid many hours of arguments, we attempted many ways of managing our money. My wife even went and got a job— against my wishes. This was just more reason for us to argue, because now she had what she called *her money*. This did not work because we had the same problem, just with more money. She would still spend money the way she wanted to without discussing it with me, and I would budget the money without discussing with her.

After her getting a job did not fix our problems, my wife attempted to manage our money. This did not work because she was not used to not being able to pay all the bills. Unfortunately, we had more bills than money, so it took a mathematician and a magician to manage our bills— someone who was great with calculations, and someone who could do magic tricks with money. I know; our money situation was a mess.

My wife was used to having money to pay all the bills, so she called every company and paid them exactly what we owed them. Where do they do that at? When she was finished, we had no money for food, gas, or our pockets. She was so upset and did not understand what just happened. This was catastrophic. I was shaking my head, knowing we were in trouble; she quickly threw the money management responsibility back to me. Now, we were back to where we started. The arguments got worse, and the money situation did not get better. We had arrived at a point where we knew that if we did not make a major change, we knew our marriage would not survive.

Around this same time, my coworker introduced me to the greatest money management program in the world: Financial Peace University (FPU) by Dave Ramsey. This program changed our lives and saved our marriage. I heard him listening to this program at work one day, and he shared with me some of the things he had taught him to do. Knowing the condition our marriage was in financially, I was willing to try anything. I went out and purchased the program immediately; it was on sale, by the way. I did not like paying full price for anything. I began listening to it on my own at first, and one day, my wife overheard some of the things Dave Ramsey was teaching and began to listen with me. Before we knew it, we were fully engaged in the FPU program. We began to see what he was saying was possible and began to apply them to our lives; it worked! It actually worked! For the first time ever in our marriage, we were actually able to work together to pay our bills, save, and get out of debt.

Now, I know I cannot share with you everything Dave Ramsey taught us; you need to go get his books and buy his program. I will share with you enough to encourage you to go get his program. I will share with you the top three steps that changed our lives.

1. Live like no one else until you can live like no one else.

Lesson 9

    2.   Spend all your money on paper before you spend it in reality.

    3.   The envelope system.

    4.   Pay God First.

Live like no one else until you can live like no one else:

Dave Ramsey explained to us the major problem in America is that everyone is trying to live beyond their means, trying to live a life they cannot afford. That was our problem. We were buying things we could not afford, just to prove to people we were living the life. We were depressing ourselves trying to impress others. He taught us that concept of living like no one else, so that one day we would be able to live like no one else.

When Dave Ramsey made this statement, what he was saying to us was that we may need to live a life with less pleasures, until we could afford to live a life full of pleasures. When we heard this, we agreed; we had been living a life we could not afford. After taking Dave Ramsey's course, we began living like no one else. We cut off cable, stopped eating out, stopped going places everyone else was going and stopped wasting money on stuff we could not afford. It was a struggle at first, but it was helping us get to a place where we could afford the lifestyle we wanted to live.

We took this extra money and put it toward paying off our Conn's bill. For those who don't know what Conn's is, it is a company that sells home appliances. We began paying double on our bill, until we paid it off. We now took that money and put it toward another bill until we paid that bill off. We continued this until we only had only our student loans, car, and house payments. This worked— we could not believe it!

Spending all your money on paper before you spend it in reality!

Living like no one else until you can live like no one else would have never worked if we never implemented the budget system Dave taught us. We learned how to spend every dime on paper— I mean every dime. The day before we received any money, we sat down together and agreed (together) where every dime was going to go when we got paid. It was frustrating, but we decided to argue twice a month instead of arguing every day of the month. After a while, we learned the rhythm of our spending, and the arguments were not as much of an issue as they were early on.

We discussed everything we would spend money on, from house bills to our blow money. Yes, we budgeted the money we would waste. We understood that if we told our money what to do, our money could never tell us what we could not do. We were finally in control of our financial future— we finally had a financial future!

Lesson 9

We budgeted for Christmas, vacations, and other important events in our lives we knew we would need extra money for. We were in the best financial place we had ever been in since we married.

Envelope System:

The envelope system complemented the budgeting system. We would have never succeeded in the budget if we did not follow the envelope system. This system was designed to help individuals use the debit card less frequently. The less often the debit card is used, the less opportunity there will be for mistakes or going over the budget.

This is how the envelope system works. After you complete the budget, there are things you will classify as cash payments; things such as groceries, gas, hair, clothes, blow money, tithes, and all the bills that could be paid in cash. Once you tallied the total, we would go to the bank and withdraw that amount. We would ask the teller to give us the number of envelopes needed to separate the money accordingly. We then would pay for everything in cash, making sure we did not go over using the debit card. This caused us, on many separate occasions, to have to put things back when we were checking out in the grocery store line. It was embarrassing, but we were living like no one else until we could live like no one else.

Putting God First:

The final lesson I will share with you that I learned from Dave is to put God first. My wife and I were faithful tithers, but at times, we would sacrifice our tithes to pay our bills. We understood that this was not good; it was like not paying our insurance. If you're a tither, you know what I am talking about. It seemed that as soon as we missed a tithe payment, everything began to go wrong. It wasn't that God was punishing us; it was as if he removed his protection. We knew we needed to pay our tithes, but we did not know how to choose our tithes over letting our lights go off. We did not know how to fully trust God.

Dave Ramsey even taught us how to put God first. The first line on his budget was tithes/charitable donations; he understood the power of sowing and reaping. Following his example, we budgeted our tithes first before we paid anything; we gave God his 10%. Let me explain something: you may not believe in paying tithes, but I want you to know it makes a difference. Since we began to pay our tithes first, we have faced hard times, but we have not gone without. God always provides. When it comes to God, you can't explain everything he does; you must have faith and trust Him, and that is what Dave Ramsey helped us do.

I can continue to teach you many other lessons we learned from Mr. Ramsey, but that is why he created his program— so you

Lesson 9

can go get it and learn it on your own. One thing I will tell you is this: my marriage would have never survived without it. We are so much better now with it. I want you to understand, once again, FPU did not wipe away all our money problems, but it did make them much better. If you're looking for perfection, this book will not help you. If you're looking to mature to survive your marriage, you're reading the right book.

Lesson 10
Parenting Is a Partnership!

So far, I have given nine different lessons my wife and I used to help us survive our marriage. I don't know if you noticed, but none of these lessons involved our children. The reason our children were not included in the lessons I shared so far is because these lessons were ways we survived our marriage or avoided getting a divorce. Early in our marriage, our children were not causing us to want to separate; as a matter of fact, our children were the reason we stayed together. So many times, we wanted to leave each other, but we looked at the children God blessed us with and did not want them to be disrupted like we were. We were both raised in homes with stepparents. Even though we turned out okay, we wanted to do our best not to put our children through that if we could avoid it.

By no means am I telling anyone to stay together for the children; that is the last thing I want you to do. No child needs their parents fighting, hating, and hurting each other on their behalf. So, I would never suggest this for anyone, but I would suggest that you use your children as a reason to fight for your marriage. If you don't have any other reason to try to work it out, your children are a good reason. That is why my wife and I tell couples, when we sit down with them to help them survive their marriage, that we do not care about them as individuals; we care about the marriage. What we are saying is that when they forget about everything that will be affected by their separation, we keep them in mind. We are fighting to keep them together on behalf of their children, family, friends, and everything connected to their relationship.

Even though our children didn't cause any issues between my wife and I early on, as they grew up, that changed quickly. As they grew up, we noticed our arguments seemed to include our children more and more. Even though we used our kids as a reason to fight to stay together, we did not want our kids to be the reason we were fighting. To avoid these scenarios, we had to come together and agree on a few things. We realized that in order to survive our marriage, we had to become a united front against our kids. No matter how upset we would get with one another, we had to realize our kids needed to see a united front. If they did not see a united front, they would find a way to use our separation of thoughts against us to get what they wanted.

First Agreement:

Lesson 10

The first thing we agreed never to do was argue in front of our children. We did not realize how dangerous this was until about four years ago. My wife was working hard to lose weight as she was having some very serious health issues. To support her efforts, I made it a point to push her to do what she needed to do to stay healthy, not matter how mad she became with me. It was nothing for me to tell her in front of the girls, "Baby, you don't need to eat that." At times, this would cause her to get upset with me and snap back. We would get upset and not speak to each other for a while. We knew this was harmless, but we did not realize how it was affecting our daughters.

One day, my oldest daughter was washing dishes and I was getting on to her about something. I cannot remember what exactly, but I noticed she had an attitude. I asked her what her problem was, and she told me never mind. Getting angry, because I felt her disrespectfully pushing me off, I told her to speak her mind. My daughter proceeded to say, "Daddy, you're always fussing about something, like you're always fussing at Momma about what she eats." Knowing my wife was sitting there listening, she figured she would support her since she was supporting my wife. My wife, as shocked as I was, looked at me with the most confused look in the world.

I got up, walked away, and immediately became angry with my wife and child. I felt as though they were partnering up against me. In that moment, I felt very disrespected. I now know that my daughter was using something against me she did not understand to support her case. She was not thinking about the issues she was creating between my wife and I; she was only trying to win leverage against me to make her point. Honestly, I should not have been upset with her. Her response was only a reflection of what she heard my wife and I argue about in front of her. I gave her the ammunition she used against me. If we had never argued in front of her, she would have never had the opportunity to use my wife as leverage against me.

That day, we learned that arguing in front of our children put them in the middle of our issues. My wife and I agreed, that day, to do our best to never again put them in our marital issues. We get upset at times and even begin to share our frustrations, but before it goes too far, we do our best to stop each other. In those moments where we are unable to restrain ourselves, we have a discussion with our children afterward, letting them know what is going on. We also let them know we are okay, and they have nothing to worry about. If they have questions, we answer them, wanting to feel as comfortable as possible after being exposed to momma and daddy's frustration with each other. They should never have to carry around our burdens.

Lesson 10

Second Agreement:

==My wife and I had to also agree never to intervene when we would be getting on one of the children.== The children can tell when their parents do not agree on something. At times, my wife felt as though I was too hard on our kids. Even though she may have been right, she could not express this in front of the kids.

My wife and I did not realize the influence we had on my daughters. We would get on to our daughters about certain things they did and, at time, one of us would make little gestures or sigh in disagreement. We thought they were harmless gestures, until our daughters started responding the same way when we brought these issues up to them in the future. We did not realize we were causing an attitude to develop in our children against the opposing parent. We were silently telling our children that we did not agree with the other parent's decision, and it was ok for them to disagree in their own way.

The first time I noticed this was when I was getting on to my oldest daughter, and she looked at my wife as if to get her approval of the command I had just delivered. Once again, I was livid. I wanted to grab her and assure her that I wasn't anything to play with. Unfortunately, it wasn't her fault. My wife did not even notice that she had nurtured that type of attitude in my daughter.

We witnessed it again, sometime later, with my middle daughter. I would always tell my daughter how she reminded me of myself with her intelligence. We would joke at times that we were the two smartest people in our home. I would even suggest, at times, that we both were smarter than her mom. I did not mean anything by it; I was only joking. Well, it wasn't funny when my wife was trying to tell her something, and my daughter responded to her like she was the dumbest person in the world.

These two different instances let us know we had to be very careful with the perceptions we gave to our daughters about each other. We realized that we had to become a team even against our kids. We could never let our children see or prey on our weak sides. We learned how to correct one another later in the privacy of our bedroom. If one of us said something the other did not agree with, we would wait until we were in the privacy of our own bedroom and ask for a truth moment. You remember truth moments, don't you? We would ask for a truth moment, discuss it, and come to an agreed upon decision on how things should have gone.

Third Agreement:

The older our daughters become, the more life moved faster than we were prepared for. School events, friend requests, and our daughter's desires became decisions for us. It was nothing for one of

Lesson 10

us to make twenty or thirty decisions before we had the opportunity to sit down and come to an agreed upon approach to a certain situation. This seems harmless, until things are being done that the other partner does not agree with. You will look up and the two of you will be upset with one another because of harmless decisions being made on the fly. No harm was intended; they were just quick decisions.

The decisions you make without your spouse can seem so small; decisions such as where the kids can and can't go, what the kids can and cannot wear, or what the kids can and cannot do. You don't even notice how these quick decisions are beginning to create a new normal in your home. You never raised kids before; you are only responding the best way you can. You don't notice how your spouse is not agree with how things are turning out. They are trying to keep it to themselves, not wanting to cause a problem over something so small. Unfortunately, what was once small will quickly turn into something big.

Take my advice: I don't care how long you have been married and how many decisions have been made, stop now and talk. First, ask your spouse if they are ok with how things are turning out with the kids. Ask them if you have made any decisions that they were not okay with. Be willing to accept "no" for an answer. If they say no, be willing to come to an agreed upon approach to parenting. If you're the one who feels as though decisions have been made without you, go to your spouse in a way that they can hear your heart. If you feel as though it is hard to discuss things like this with them, seek professional help from a mediator. It is important to come to an agreement about the kids. If you don't, your kids will cause you to hate one another.

If you have young kids, I suggest you begin to talk now about future decisions. Prior to our kids growing up, my wife and I decided on a few things they will and will not do:

1. They will not stay at anyone's home we do not know.
2. They will not wear makeup until seventh grade.
3. They will not wear anything that either one of us views as disrespectful.
4. They will go to church as long as they live in our home.

We made these decisions and more before our daughters even started walking. Now that they are older, we have made some adjustments, but it is easier to adjust than it is to create on the fly. Don't put yourself in that situation, if you can avoid it. The last thing you want to do is argue about your kids. Do whatever you can to avoid doing this.

A Message to My Blended Families:

Lesson 10

Let me stop for a moment and address my blended families, the couples who were married and had kids prior to the relationship. Listen to me very closely; what I am about to tell you could save you a lot of trouble in the future. I know it is hard parenting another person's child, but it can work if the two of you agree not to take everything the other does so personal. Remember this...

Fathers, remember that mothers are going to be mothers. Mothers are protective of their children, no matter who you are. This is just the nature of a mother, and it has nothing to do with the fact that you're not the children's father. My wife is protective of my daughters against me. I understand how you feel, but I promise you it has nothing to do with the fact that you're not the children's father.

Mothers, fathers will be fathers. I know it appears as if he is being harder on your children than he is being on his children. Don't take it personal. The reason he is being harder on your children is because his children already know what he expects. He feels as though he needs to get them to understand him, and he does not realize he is focusing on your children more than his.

Finally, both of you need to understand that children will be children. Children will do their best to get what they want at any cost. My children come against me as well as my wife. However, we must stay a team, and I say the same to the two of you: stay a team. I also suggest you never say to one another, "you handle your kids, and I will handle mine." The kids deserve to be loved by both of you, and that is what discipline is. The kids will respond much worse to you if you reject them than they will if you discipline them.

Whether you're a blended family, or a traditional family, you must remember this statement: "Together we stand, divided we fall."

Lesson 11
His Needs, Her Needs!

Lesson number Eleven. Wow, we are almost at the end of this book. Can I stop for a moment and tell you how I thank God that he has allowed me the opportunity to come this far? This is my first book. My wife has motivated me to do this, and I am almost at the end. I thank God for her. I remember when I was the one who motivated her to do everything; now, she is my role model. I want you to know that just writing this book has helped me, so I pray reading it has helped you.

I learned the first nine lessons of this book during the first nine years of our relationship. Those were the hardest nine years of our lives. We had some good and some bad times, but through it all, we survived. We started pastoring around the 10th year of our marriage. During this time, we had reached a pretty good place in our relationship. For the first five years of ministry, we were so focused on building our ministry from the ground up that we did not have time to argue about much. God knew we had to mature quickly because we were going to need to minister to other marriages and families.

We spent the next five years sharing with other people what we learned in the first nine years of our marriage. It was as if God put our marriage on pause, knowing there were more important things we needed to address. I must say that it was a relief knowing everything we had gone through was not in vain. We were able to do so much for so many people. During our time with the people we were helping, we were helped all over again. It was as if we were recycling the lessons we had already learned and learning how to use them all over again as we shared them with other people.

We did learn some new lessons during this time, but that will be published in our next book titled, "Team Harden: Marriage Survival Guide part II". The subtitle will be, "How we Survived our Marriage in Ministry." The lesson we learned during this time was not the same as the lessons we learned during our first nine years of marriage; they were more isolated to church and ministry. I pray this next book helps save many marriages that are suffering from the pains of ministry.

After the first five years of ministry were over, it was as if God took the blinders off. The church was up and functioning properly. We had leaders to help us lead, and we finally came to a point where we were spending more time at home than we were at church. We

Lesson 11

learned quickly that working in ministry caused a few issues that we were unaware of. These were not issues that were ministry related as much as they were related to two people being very busy. I know many of you can relate to this. I was beginning to feel very neglected, and my wife had started to feel the same way. We don't know why, but in our fourteen years of marriage, we never remembered feeling that way before.

I began to tell my wife how I needed sex. I was used to people complaining about their wives not giving them any, but this was never an issue for me. I was getting very angry, thinking that I was no longer a priority on her list of responsibilities. I was becoming angry, to the point where I would even begin to think about why I was married if my wife was not going to handle the one thing we had been doing from the beginning. We had recently stopped masturbating as well. This did not make it any better.

Side note: Yep, I said we stopped masturbating. We learned that we were going to set the example. We were going to wait for one another. We felt that if we masturbated, we might as well have laid with another person. We did not need each other sexually if we took care of ourselves. As a result, our sex life increased so much because we waited.

Even though our sex life increased because of the lack of masturbation, we had arrived at a drought during this time, in my mind. My wife was not too happy during this time. She began using statements like, "You're treating me like a piece of meat." I did not understand what she meant. She would say that all I wanted to do was touch and fondle on her when I wanted sex. I was confused; I thought that was the way I let her know I wanted sex. She was angry with me, and I was angry with her. We didn't fully understand why we were angry with one another, and we were in a bad place once again. We would walk around the house frustrated. That was the only word that could express our feelings: frustrated. We were not mad because we knew the other person did not understand. We were frustrated because the other person did not understand.

One day, I heard about this book titled, *His Need, Her Needs*. It sounded like a great marriage book to share with our marriage ministry. To help our church couples, we started teaching this class together. Little did we know, the impact this class would have on our marriage would be substantial. This book took our entire marriage and redefined it in six months. We thought we knew it all. Here we were, thinking since everybody was coming to us for help, we had it all figured out. After reading this book, we learned quickly how we were going about everything all wrong when it came to getting what we wanted or needed from each other.

I guess that early on in our relationship, we took each other for granted. We did not have very many demands. If I wanted sex, my wife would just say yes. If my wife wanted me to do something

Lesson 11

for her, she just asked. I guess we had become so busy where things were not so natural anymore. All of a sudden, our needs were taken care of so seldom that we noticed something was wrong, but we could not put our finger on it. All we knew was we felt neglected. For the first time in fourteen years, it was time to focus on each other needs.

The book taught us this: if we planned to live a happy life, we had to understand that his needs and her needs are different. The busier you become with kids, work, ministry, family, and hobbies, the harder it is to meet these needs. This is when you must sit down and understand each other's needs and meet them purposely. If not, you will end up shutting down on each other, causing each other to become frustrated. Frustration can lead to separation. Remember, we're trying to help you survive your marriage. Therefore, we need to avoid frustration at all costs.

In the first chapter, we learned the importance of not only knowing each other's needs, but how the most important thing was to know our own needs. The problem with most relationships is that the frustrated person does not even know what they want. They just know they are tired of making you happy and not being happy in return. You ever get upset because you are giving so much and not getting anything in return? Then, the other person asks you what you want them to do for you, and you reply saying, "I don't know, that's your job to find out." Well, you're wrong: it's your job to tell them. They only know what they need; they don't know what you need.

This was my problem. I thought I was an expert at what my wife needed, but I did not know what I needed. I later learned that I was wrong about her needs as well. Wants and needs are different. A person can survive without wants, but they cannot survive without needs. After reading the book, I learned quickly that I needed stuff like:

1. Validation
2. Physical touch
3. To be needed
4. To be appreciated
5. Sex

I figured sex would have been in the top three, but it wasn't. If my wife tried to meet my top three needs, she could not have because I did not even know what they were. After analyzing my needs, I then analyzed my wife's needs. Wow, I never knew my wife's number one need was security; knowing that we were going to be okay financially. I thought it was compassion, me spending time with her and listening to her talk. That was like number four. The reason we were so frustrated with one another is because we did not know what we needed, or what each other needed.

Lesson 11

This book then taught us how we should now focus on taking care of the other person's needs, never caring about our own. The trick is to focus on their need, no matter what. It is a plus if they return the favor, but real love is when you focus all on their needs and they focus on yours. After about a week of doing this, our marriage was blown away. It was like getting soda out of a soda machine. I took care of my wife, and she took care of me. My wife took care of me, and I took care of her. It was amazing an overnight change.

Now, I would love to be able to tell you that we continued down this road of success for ever, but that is not the case. We got lazy every now and then, but I can admit that being exposed to our problem was much more rewarding than getting our needs meet. We can now quickly recognize when we are getting to the point where we are neglecting to take care of one another. My advice to each of you would be:

1. **Listen to your bodies:** If you're feeling neglected, chances are that you're being neglected. You must speak up. Even though they are supposed to take care of your needs, it's not as easy as it seems. Their needs seem to be at the top of their list. You must let it be known that your needs are not being meet. Ignoring them will create frustrations, and remember, frustration leads to separation.

2. **Listen to your spouse**: No matter how much you think you know, you don't know your spouse like your spouse know themselves. Remember Chapter Seven: It's Too Late, They Already Feel it. Well, no matter how wrong you think they are, if they say you're not meeting their needs, you're not meeting their needs. If you continue to neglect their needs, they may find someone else to meet them. If they do, you will only have yourself to blame.

3. **Stop being so busy**: We must slow down, both as individuals and couples. If you're too busy and your spouse tells you to slow down, slow down. They are saying you're doing too much and neglecting your responsibilities. The problem is bad when both of you are busy. My wife and I have fallen victim to this problem on many different occasions. We will look up, and a week has gone by while we have neglected each other. The problem with this is that we will forfeit our own needs to complete a project. I would not push my wife, and my wife would not push me. Both of us would neglect ourselves, and each other. This is not healthy for any relationship. Ignoring each other could lead to infidelity, because ignoring the need does not make the need go away.

  I can, by no means, summarize in a single chapter what the book *His Needs, Her Needs* has given my wife and I, so my recommendation is for you to pick that book up after you complete these books my wife and I wrote for you. We recommend this book to every couple. Your needs are important; never forget that.

Lesson 12
Team Harden

Team Harden— what does this mean? Where did it come from? How did it save our marriage? These are all legitimate questions but let me start off by telling you this: there would have never been a book, church, or marriage if we did not find Team Harden. Team Harden is more than a name; it is a thought. During our worst times, we know that no matter what, we have Team Harden.

This whole concept was developed in our time of ministry. Once again, this will be in our next book as well, *How we Survived our Marriage in Ministry*. I am sharing a snippet of the concept with you because you need to know this lesson outside of ministry. Many of you may have businesses that you're working in together, and if you're not careful, it could tear you apart— that is what ministry almost did to us.

When we began ministry together, I was very naïve. I was so focused on getting the church together that I was not focused on anything else. My wife would come to me and inform me of so many things that I would not see. If I did not see it, in my mind, it did not exist. No matter how many times she would tell me what people were doing, or how they did not have our best interests at heart, I would ignore her. I made her feel very isolated, to the point to where she felt as though it was me and the church against her.

We got into so many arguments, and she threatened to leave the church on so many occasions. I remembered times where I saw what she was talking about, but I would try to ignore them, hoping that they would go away. I would ignore them and tell her that it wasn't that bad, or I would tell her she was making things look worse than they were. This put a large wedge between my wife and me. It created areas in our relationship that we could not talk about. I did not know how dangerous this was for my marriage. If my wife could not talk to me about something that was so important to me, who was she supposed to talk to? It literally was me and the church against her. It was almost like another woman.

Let me bring it to a place you may understand. While the church was my *thing*, your *thing* may take a different form. It may be your mother, your business, your family, or even your baby's mother. It can be anything that means the world to you, or something that is connected to you that you cannot easily get rid of. It may have been there before your spouse, or it may be there after your spouse. To keep down confusion, you attempt to deflect whatever issues are

Lesson 12

going on. In your mind, you believe the less friction, the better. You want everyone to just get along.

Well, that is how I was with the church and other things. I did not realize how much it was affecting my marriage. The worst part was that I did not realize how much it was affecting the church I was defending. The church was not just a building. The church was people. Like I said before, your mother, your baby momma, the people on your job. I wasn't defending a building against my wife; I was defending other women against my wife. This was not just isolated to church. Any woman who came to me needing help, I was naive to the fact that they may have wanted to be with me. I would think they only wanted me to minister to them. My wife would do her best to warn me if she sensed the intentions of these women were different, but I told her it was my job. In my mind, she was just being jealous. How could she fight against ministry? How can your spouse fight against the mother of your child, or your mother not liking her? This fight made her look bad and made her feel crazy.

This frustration went on for months, until all hell broke loose one day. I will spare you the details. Just believe me when I tell you I saw what my wife had been trying to tell me for years. This was the third time a situation like this occurred, where my wife was telling me something that I did not believe, and it backfired in my face. Finally, I saw the light for what it was. I could not believe that I put her through years of hell. For the first time, I saw something I never realized before. My wife was not only looking out for herself or me; she was looking out for our name. She was protecting the Harden name. I also realized that she saw things that I could not see. I knew then that if we were going to survive out here, we had to become a team. I had to have her back against the world, and she had to have mine. I approached my wife with a deep apology. I told her that I hated how I made her feel for so long, and how I should have listened to her years ago before things got as bad as they did. I assured her that from now on, I would listen to her, and we would forever be, "TEAM HARDEN". It was us against the world.

That day, I realized my wife could see things about me that I could not see, and I could see things about her that she could not see. If I chose to spend the rest of my life with her, I had to start trusting her with my life. I had to trust that she had my best interest at heart. She did this because she knew when I won, she won and when she won, I won. No matter what, it was Team Harden on the line.

I had never felt that I could trust anyone like this before. I thought I had to protect myself against everyone. No one ever told me I don't have to protect myself against my own wife. Let me tell you something: if you don't trust your spouse, fix it. Go to counselling, go get help. Do whatever you have to do to understand one another. I told you earlier in this book that we both were in this hole called marriage, and the only way we're going to get out is together. If you ever plan to survive this hole, you must learn how to work together.

Lesson 12

Marriage is always attacking, or should I say something is always attacking your marriage. Money, family, friends, children, sickness, debt, depression, the past, and the future are all working against you. You have two choices: you can let it destroy you, or you can come together as a team and fight back. My wife and I have decided to fight back. We even fight against each other if we are doing something that will destroy team Harden. We fight each other to stay healthy, holy, humble, and hungry. We must always continue to get better. We are lifelong partners in life. Together we stand, divided we fall.

I did not realize how hard I made it on my wife. Once we began working together as a team, I did see how much happier she became. Once again, she could tell me anything. It was no longer me and the church against her; it was me and her against the church. She wasn't trying to destroy the church; she was trying to stop me from destroying the church and our name, Team Harden.

I pray each of the lessons I have shared with you in this book is as much of a blessing to you as it was to us. We are seventeen years in, and we plan to go many more years. We don't know what the future has in store for us, but we pray that the lessons we learned up until this point in our marriage helps you survive yours.

Do me a favor: if this book blessed your marriage, share it with someone else. Let's save marriages everywhere.

To book Team Harden to speak to your ministry or organization about this book and more,

Call: 936-653-4525

Email: bishopharden@ndfcworldchangers.org

Email: ladyharden@ndfcworldchangers.org

Or visit our website: www.ndfcworldchangers.org

Lesson 12

Made in the USA
Lexington, KY
02 July 2018